P9-DEY-277

Persistent.....43
The Evolutionary Tree.....44
Fossils at the Burgess Shale are
    Different.....46

Animals Found at the Burgess Shale are
    Seen with Variation Later.....46
Let's See if We Can Make a Short
    Summary.....47

Episode #53 – *Journey into the Blast Zone – Part I* *48*

Job 12:7-9

Job 12:7-9.....48
Eruption of Mount St. Helens......48

Rapid Layering.....52
Rapid Carving of Canyons.....53

Episode #54 – *Journey into the Blast Zone – Part II* *54*

Genesis 8:17

Rapid Recovery.....54
Rapid Deposit of Logs.....56
Yellowstone.....57
Log Jam Game.....60
Dating a Lava Dome Rock.....63

Evolution's Objections to Our
    Conclusions.....65
Creation Rebuttal.....65
Why is this Important.....66

Episode #55 – *The Artic Adventure – Part I* *67*

Genesis 1:20-21

Ellesmere Island.....67
What is a Tetrapod?.....68
A First Look at Tiktaalik.....68
Classification of Fish.....70

Mosaic Creatures.....73
Evolution's Problem of Time.....76
Color the Mosaic.....77

Episode #56 – *The Artic Adventure – Part II* *78*

Romans 1:20

The Fin 'Progression'.....78
Morphological Sequence......79
Geologic Sequence.....80

A Summary.....82
Evolution of a Car.....83
Crossword Puzzle.....84

Episode #57 – *The Journey into the Deep – Part I* 85

Job 40:31

Juan de Fuca Ridge…..85
The Law of Biogenesis…..86
Traffic Laws & the Laws of Science…..88
Evolutionary Origin of Life Theories…..89
Black Smokers and Evolution…..91
The Black Smokers and the Life Found There…..93

Animals Adapted to the Life in the Deep Hotness!!.....94
Chemosynthesis…..95
Designed Adaptation…..96
Activity……96
Recipe for Gooo!.....97

Episode #58 – *The Journey into the Deep – Part II* 98

Hebrews 1:3

Origin of Life Dilemmas…..98
Origin of Life Experiments…..100
Miller-Urey Experiment…..101
Sidney Fox Experiment…..102

Geologic Evidence for Oxygen…..103
Difference Between Creation and Evolution Perspectives…..104
Ephesians 6:10-15……105

Episode #59 – *The Final Battle – Part I* 106

Genesis 7:17-20

What Killed the Dinosaurs?......107
Dinosaur Extinction……108
What are Fossil Graveyards?.....109
Water Has Power!......110

Activity: Testing Turbulence……111
Difference Between Evolution Model and Creation……112
The Dwarf Dinosaurs…..113

Episode #60 – *The Final Battle – Part II* 116

Psalm 139

The Bare Bones…..116
Where do Creation and Evolution Differ?.....117
Interclasts…..117

Carbonate Mudstone…..118
Variety of Animals…..119
Matching Game…..121
Fill in the Blank…..122

Getting the Most From This Study Guide

The Jonathan Park Audio Adventures were produced to help children and families have a strong foundation on which to build their faith! Unfortunately, many live as if their belief in the Bible is just another brand of religion. However, God has given us a gift that we often take for granted – He has asked us to believe in truth! Sadly, many Christians are intimidated by evolutionary ideas and told that the Word of God has been disproven by science. The truth is that if God really created the universe, animals, and mankind like He said in Genesis, we should be able to investigate this world and find evidence that what He says is true… and we do!

Think about the difference between the Christian and evolutionary worldviews. If evolution is true, then there is no God and we are the product of random evolutionary processes. As nothing more than a bunch of molecules, we have no purpose in life. On the other hand, if we were created, it means that we were made especially by a loving Creator who has a unique purpose for each of our lives! This difference can completely change a person's life! Truly knowing that God's Word is true is a foundation that will change every aspect of a child's life. That's what we hope to accomplish with the Jonathan Park project – to teach families about scientific evidence that is in harmony with God's Word.

We've designed the audio adventures so families can enjoy them in their cars – while on trips or just running errands. They can listen at home or during family devotional time. Our goal is to provide exciting adventures that run deep with creation apologetics and Biblical lessons. We hope that you enjoy them regardless of where you listen to them!

This Jonathan Park Study Guide has been designed to maximize teaching from each episode in the Jonathan Park Series. Our hope is that after listening to each Jonathan Park Audio Adventure, parents will sit down with their children and work through the information provided in this booklet. Here's how we recommend you use this guide with your child:

1. Listen to an episode from the Jonathan Park: The Explorers' Society - Album #5.
2. Begin your study by praying with your child. Pray that God will teach you truth and continue to build your faith.
3. In the Table of Contents, we've listed Scripture references for each episode. Spend time reading through this section of God's Word.
4. Next, open this Study Guide to the corresponding section. The information is arranged in bite-

sized nuggets – each builds upon the previous one. Read through the information with your child and relate it back to the Word of God.

5. Let the child ask questions, and help them find answers. This Study Guide may be the key to unlocking doubts that a child has. Always follow up a child's question. Refer to other creation science resources, or make a commitment to search for the answer together. These questions are excellent ways to take them deeper into God's Word.

6. End in prayer. Thank the Lord for the specific things He has taught during this time.

While this Study Guide is designed to address *scientific* issues, we have also created devotionals that focus on the *Biblical* aspect of the topics presented on each episode of Jonathan Park. In addition, we have also prepared Real Adventures – activities that can be used to reinforce the information within this booklet. For these devotionals and activities, go to www.JonathanPark.com and click on "Real Adventures".

"But sanctify the Lord God in your hearts: and be ready always to give an answer to every man that asketh you a reason of the hope that is in you with meekness and fear."

- I Peter 3:15

Did you know that the study of many branches of our present day sciences were founded by scientists who believed in the Bible? Here are a few of them:

Robert Boyle-Chemistry

Johan Kepler-Astronomy

John Ray-Biology

Mathew Maury-Oceanography

The study of most of these sciences only began a few hundred years ago. When you think of this in terms of all of history, the formal study of science is pretty young.

Timeline of four sciences

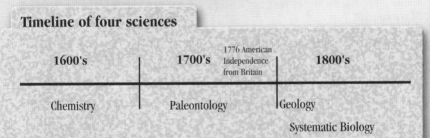

1600's	1700's	1776 American Independence from Britain	1800's
Chemistry	Paleontology	Geology	
			Systematic Biology

As you can see from the timeline, the study of three of the four sciences on the line began about the same time that America gained independence from Britain. Since that time, there have been many new theories presented in each of these fields. One of those theories within the science of Geology began about 200 years ago and was called the theory of uniformity.

Uniformitarianism

Have you and your siblings ever worn a matching outfit? Or have you ever been on a sports team where you all wore the same jersey or t-shirt? This is called a uniform.

The word uniform means never changing or all alike.
A uniform pattern means the pattern stays the same or does not vary.

Notice the straight line drawn below:

This is a uniformly straight line.

Notice the next line below:

The pattern of peaks and dips on this line is also uniform.
The peaks could represent a natural disaster like a volcano or an earthquake. For example, about 50 - 60 volcanoes erupt each year. Likewise, there is usually a magnitude eight earthquake each year.

Some scientists claim that the uniform repetition of these natural events is how the earth was formed, and that everything that happens in the present, also happened in the same way in the past. This is called the theory of Uniformitarianism, and was first published by a man named James Hutton and later popularized by Charles Lyell. A key phrase used by scientists that ascribe to this theory is "the present is the key to understanding the past."

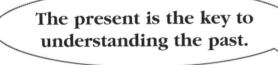

The present is the key to understanding the past.

Charles Lyell

Here's an example of how this theory works:

Uniformitarinists once believed that the Grand Canyon was slowly, uniformly carved by a river flowing over the same area for long periods of time. Now there is great evidence that this idea was wrong. Niagara Falls has had a similar theory explaining how Niagara gorge was formed.

Niagara Falls

Four million cubic feet of water flow over the falls every minute. It is the most powerful waterfall in North America.

It is a set of three waterfalls: American falls, Bridal Veil Falls, and Horseshoe falls.

Horseshoe Falls is 2,600 feet wide 170 foot drop.

It borders US and Canada and is a 20 minute drive from Buffalo, NY and 1 1/2 hours from Toronto, Ontario Canada. Currently between 50% and 75% of the Niagara River's flow is diverted by four huge tunnels that start far upstream from the waterfalls. The water passes through turbines that supply power to the United States and Canada before returning to the river past the Falls.

Charles Lyell traveled to Niagara Falls to find evidence to support the uniformity theory. He tried to find the age of the falls and calculated it to be 35,000 years old.

Is this age older than the Biblical age of the earth?
Yes it is.

Because of that fact, when Lyell published his findings it caused people to doubt the Bible.

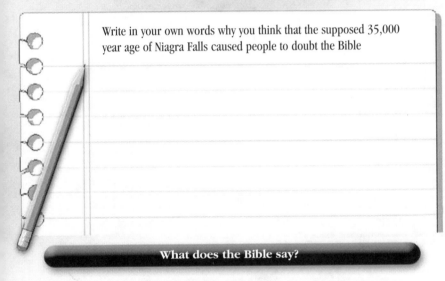

Write in your own words why you think that the supposed 35,000 year age of Niagra Falls caused people to doubt the Bible

What does the Bible say?

Even though every specific scientific fact is not found in the Bible, it does not mean that the Bible is wrong or incomplete. There are many scientific truths mentioned in the Bible in which we can gain wisdom.

Can you find at least three verses in the Bible that talk about some kind of science or scientific fact? Hint: Be sure to check out Job!

1. _____
2. _____
3. _____

II Peter 3:3-7 actually seems to talk about the uniformitarian idea:

> "Knowing this first, that there shall come in the last days scoffers, walking after their own lusts, And saying, Where is the promise of his coming? for since the fathers fell asleep, all things continue as they were from the beginning of the creation. For this they willingly are ignorant of, that by the word of God the heavens were of old, and the earth standing out of the water and in the water: Whereby the world that then was, being overflowed with water, perished: But the heavens and the earth, which are now, by the same word are kept in store, reserved unto fire against the day of judgment and perdition of ungodly men."

It says that people will scoff about Christ's return, saying that <u>all things continue as they were from the beginning.</u> They have willingly forgotten that God created and then flooded the earth.

THE POINT IS that the Bible warns us of people who believe that everything continues as it has from the beginning, without any special intervention by the Creator. Here are some lessons we can learn from the situation of Charles Lyell and the old age he came up with for Niagara Falls.

1. Some Christians doubted the Bible because of the news about the age of the falls. However, we need to remember that headlines are often exaggerated and the information often tainted by opinion rather than fact, so do your own research before jumping to conclusions.

2. The Bible is the truth. When a 'new discovery' seems to contradict the Bible, it is usually best to - wait and see, because in the end the Bible will always been shown to be reliable. Charles Lyell's age of 35,000 years was 'proven wrong' long ago.

Rate of Erosion

Do you know what a rate is from studying math? How fast can you ride your bike? The measurement of this is a rate.

Do you remember learning about erosion? It is the wearing away, in this case, of the earth by water.

When Charles Lyell traveled to Niagara Falls to find out how old they were, he studied the rate of erosion.

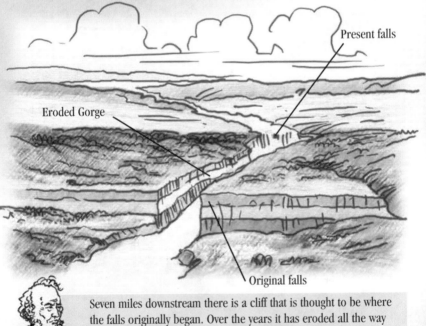

Present falls

Eroded Gorge

Original falls

Seven miles downstream there is a cliff that is thought to be where the falls originally began. Over the years it has eroded all the way back to the present location. (see drawing)

One eye-witness told Lyell that the Falls had moved 150 feet during the previous 40 years. Can you determine the rate of erosion? Let's do the math! First make the ratio as follows:

$$\frac{150 \text{ feet}}{40 \text{ years}}$$

Next, divide 150 by 40 to find how many feet per one year.

$$150 \div 40 \text{ or } 15 \div 4 = 3.75 \text{ feet per year}$$

According to this man the erosion rate of Niagara Falls was 3.75 feet per year. If we simply used this rate for determining the age of the falls, it would be 7,000 - 9,000 years old. For some reason Lyell did not use this rate, but instead claimed that it was 35,000 years old. As we will see later, neither the dates of 7,000 or 35,000 are the correct answers - it appears they are much younger!

Erosion Activity

Materials:

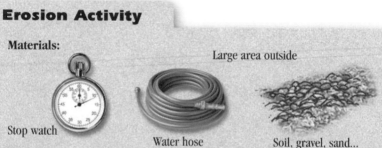

Stop watch

Large area outside

Water hose

Soil, gravel, sand...

Instructions:

With permission and supervision from your parents, construct a mound of soil. Build your mound using layers of various materials. For example layer dirt, then gravel, then sand, then more dirt, then larger gravel then maybe a piece of wood and some more dirt. Pack each layer tightly on top of the other. Next place the water hose at the top and rear of the mound. Get your stop watch ready. Turn on the hose full blast, start the stop watch and time how long it takes the water to erode a canyon in your mound of land. You may want to do several trials to see what type of mound erodes faster or slower or discover how a slower flow of water changes the rate of erosion.

The Layers at Niagara Falls

It can be observed at the Falls and along the gorge that there are different rock layers and thicknesses as you travel the length of the gorge. For example, Lockport Dolomite is a hard rock layer at the Falls, while Rochester Shale is a softer layer under the dolomite layer.

As the water flowed down the gorge, it eroded the softer shale away from under the dolomite, leaving it sticking out until it eventually broke off in large chunks.

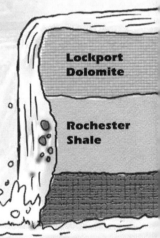

Lockport Dolomite

Rochester Shale

Did you see this happen in your erosion activity?

At the current location of the falls, the dolomite is 90 feet thick, but throughout most of the length of the gorge it thins down to only 45 feet thick.

Based on your erosion activity, how do you think different thicknesses of layers affected the erosion rate? Also, when you slowed down the water flow, did the rate of erosion slow down too? When the hose was on all the way did erosion happen faster?

> **THE POINT IS** that different factors change the rate of erosion. Niagara Falls may have actually eroded faster in the past because:
> - the amount of water changes the rate
> - the thickness of hard rock layers affects the rate

Time for some vocabulary housecleaning!

Okay, so now we give you permission to throw the age of 35,000 years old for Niagara Falls out the window!

Evolutionary scientists have even concluded that the age is much younger!

Did you know that Geologists used to call themselves uniformitarians?! You can throw that term out the window too!

So how did evolutionists conclude that the falls are 12,000 years old? Also, why do many geologists now call themselves 'actualists'? ... KEEP READING.

The evolution of uniformitarians to actualists

First let's look at the difference between an actualist geologist and a uniformitarian geologist:

Uniformist

Uniformists say that the rock layers were made only by <u>slow gradual processes.</u>

Actualist

Actualists say that the rock layers of the earth were made by <u>slow gradual processes and natural catastrophes.</u>

Many actualist geologists now say the evidence shows that natural catastrophes formed the earth and changed erosion rates. However, they are still using uniformitarian ideas when they date Niagara Falls, which they believe to be 12,000 years old.

Why do they think this?

They use carbon dating and look at the general evolutionary age of the surrounding area. First, let's look at carbon dating!

Carbon is an element in and on the earth just like oxygen, hydrogen, and nitrogen.

Carbon is represented by the letter — **C**

Nitrogen is represented by the letter — **N**

Oxygen is represented by the letter — **O**

Hydrogen is represented by the letter — **H**

Water is made up of an H, another H, and an O like this: **H_2O**

All living things take in carbon from their surroundings. (It is important to remember that only living objects, and not something like rocks, takes in carbon!) This type of carbon, the type that is measured in carbon dating, is called carbon 14 or C-14. However, when a tree, shell, or bone dies it stops taking in C-14, and the existing carbon begins to deteriorate and become nitrogen 14, or N-14.

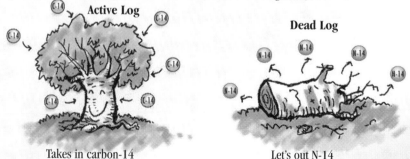

Active Log

Takes in carbon-14

Dead Log

Let's out N-14

So how does this tell you how old something is? Well, we know that when something like a tree dies, the C-14 that it took in before it died, now begins to deteriorate into N-14. If we know the rate at which this change happens, we can determine how long the tree has been dead.

SOUNDS SIMPLE???!!! Not so fast!

How can I determine the age if I don't even know how much C-14 there was to start with?

The problem is that we do not know the amount of C-14 in the environment when the plant/animal died. We can measure what it is now, but what if the amount was different in the past? In fact we know that there were different amounts of C-14 in the environment!

If we guess the wrong amount of C-14, the log will NOT be the right age. And creation scientists believe that there is good reason to believe that the amounts of C-14 were much different in the past. Although uniformitarians have a way to try to correct for these differences, their dates are still wrong if they do not assume the correct amounts of C-14 in the past (such as denying a worldwide flood).

Another Problem with Carbon dating.

-Some plants and animals take in *different* amounts of carbon. This makes them appear older or younger than they actually are.

Have you ever read the Winnie the Pooh books? There is a game that Pooh plays that is called Pooh sticks.

Materials:
One or two wood sticks per person (length can vary)
A bridge over a moving stream

Directions:
Stand on the upstream side of the bridge. Have someone say "Go!" and everyone throw their sticks into the water at the same time. Be sure to remember which stick belongs to you! Run to the other side of the bridge (the downstream side) and watch closely to see whose stick came out the other side first. That stick is the winner!

Did the same stick come out first that went under the bridge first? If not why?

When you were running from one side of the bridge to the other, could there have been something that you did not see that changed the rate of flow of the stick? What might have happened?

THE POINT IS that, like the unknown factors that may have changed the rate of flow for the stick, the same is true of the amount of C-14 in the environment. There are unknown factors that may have changed the amount of it in the atmosphere over time. So as you can see, the evolutionists may call themselves actualists, but their carbon-dating is still completely built on uniformitarianism because they trust that the rate of carbon decay is consistent.

The other dating method used by evolutionists: Gauging the age of the surrounding area:

According to evolutionists, 18,000 years ago Niagara Falls were covered by an ice sheet called the Wisconsin Glaciation. There is proof that these glaciers once existed, and that they carved out the Great Lakes and then melted making a huge flow from Lake Erie to Ontario that created the original falls. However, Creationists and Evolutionists decided the age of those glaciers very differently.

Evolutionists vs. Creationists

Evolutionists would say that the Niagara falls area was formed after the melting of the 18,000 year old Wisconsin glaciation, making the falls area about 12,000 years old

Creationists would say that the glacial period took place after the world wide flood and the falls area is less than 5,000 years ago.

All agree that the glacier in that area was like a bulldozer pushing and grinding the land. This would have made some rivers deeper, dug lakes, and forced other rivers to make new paths.

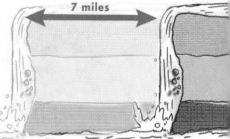

The original falls of Niagara were 7 miles downstream from their current location. The erosion of the crest of the falls has caused this retreat.

Amazingly, someday the falls could retreat far enough back to drain most of Lake Erie since the bottom of Lake Eire is higher than the bottom of the falls!

So how old are Niagara Falls anyway?

Quite a few years back engineers took several steps to stop, for the most part, the erosion at the Falls. Before that time, it was measured that they were traveling 4 - 5 feet a year. Using only this rate of erosion the falls would date to 7 - 9,000 years. However, we also found out that the hard Dolomite layer was half as thick for a long stretch of the gorge. That would cut the age way down.

It also appears that when the falls made their way to a section of the gorge, it encountered a channel of very soft material that was at a right angle from its previous course. It turned, following that soft material before continuing on its way. Some believe that this section of the gorge was carved in a matter of weeks or days instead of hundreds or thousands of years. Again, this would reduce the age of the falls.

Toward the start of the glacial melt it would be logical to assume that there was much greater water flow than we currently see on the river. This too would seem to cause a much greater rate of erosion.

Further, the current horseshoe shape of the falls is not very conducive to erosion. However, some have suggested that in the past, the falls had a notch-shape. This would erode much quicker, which would also bring down the age of the falls.

The worldwide flood would also affect the rate of erosion. Afterward, following the ice age, it would be plausible that the river contained much more sediments, and these abrasives would also have sped the rate of erosion.

There are also factors that would *slow* down the process. It is currently believed that there was a long period in which the river was temporarily redirected, slowing to 10% of its flow. This would greatly draw-out the erosion process. However, it is likely that all of the other factors outweigh this temporary decrease. In other words, our starting point of 7 - 9,000 can be whittled down much further.

So exactly how old are the Falls? If the above factors bear themselves out, then the age of Niagara Falls is much younger than 7,000 years. But at this point we have to be honest. There are so many things that still need to understand about Niagara Falls and the complex interplay of all these processes. But there is one thing we can say with confidence. The evidence from Niagara Falls has in no way stood opposed to the Biblical account as Charles Lyell once claimed. As we learn more about this fascinating area, it will - like so many other places - confirm the Genesis account!

The Big Picture

We have been looking at a little piece of the earth in Niagara Falls, so let's now zoom out and look at a bigger picture.

Evolutionary and Creationist beliefs about the age and creation process of the earth

Age:

Evolutionary age of the earth: 4.5 billion years old

Creation age of the earth: Around 6,000 years old

How it was formed:

Uniformists-slow gradual processes made the earth.

Actualists-local catastrophes and slow processes made the earth.

Creationists - After an original creation was made by God, a huge disaster flooded and molded the earth into almost what we see now.

Conclusion

So why do we study the age of the earth and the various aspects of the creation around us? Because, not only do we learn new and fascinating things about the amazing Creator God and His magnificent creation, but we are also helping to give hope to many by showing that science and the Bible are in harmony. It shows that there is a purpose and plan behind our existence! In science this is called the study of origins.

Sadly, for many who believe the lie of evolution, their origins are an accidental explosion that randomly "created" our world millions of years ago for no real reason or purpose. We're just here because....well, because. But as Christians, we know the glorious truth that God created our world, created each of us, and that He has a plan and purpose for everything and everyone. This is why we study and learn about our world: to bring glory and honor to Him and to help to testify to the truth of God's Word. So, happy studying!

Actual TRUE Facts About Niagra Falls: Its History of Daredevils!

We have almost 180 years of recorded attempts by various individuals to challenge the bounds of safety surrounding the Falls. Here are a few:

In 1829, Sam Patch, who called himself The Yankee Leaper, jumped over Horseshoe Falls and became the first known person to survive.

Jean Francois "Blondin" Gravelet in 1859, crossed the Falls on a tightrope. These tightrope walkers drew huge crowds to witness the challenge. Their wires ran across the gorge, near the current Rainbow Bridge, but not over the waterfall itself. Ontario's William Hunt competed with Blondin in performing outrageous stunts over the gorge.

Englishman Captain Matthew Webb, the first man to swim the English Channel, drowned in 1883 after unsuccessfully trying to swim across the whirlpools and rapids downriver from the Falls.

In 1901, 63-year-old Annie Edson Taylor was the first person to go over the Falls in a barrel.

Bobby Leach and his barrel after his trip over Niagara Falls, 1911

Since then, 14 other people have intentionally gone over the Falls in or on a device. Some have survived unharmed, but others have drowned or been severely injured. Survivors of such stunts face charges and fines because it is illegal to attempt to go over the Falls.

Jonathan Park

Have you ever been to Canada? The Canadian Rocky mountains are beautiful to behold. Walcott Quarry, the area that this episode takes place, is in British Colombia between the tops of Wapta Mountain and Mount Field.

Walcott Quarry was discovered in 1909 by Charles Walcott. He was the secretary for the Smithsonian Institute in Washington D.C., which is a collection of museums. He gathered thousands of fossils from this area.

As you will see, this site is claimed by both evolutionists and creationists as support for their theories. The real question will be which theory fits best?

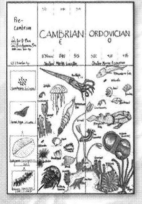

Cambrian Explosion

Cambrian is the name for the particular layer of rock in the earth's crust where creatures are found at the Walcott Quarry. This layer is not just found in Canada but in different places around the world.

The Cambrian explosion is called an explosion because at this point in the fossil record there is a sudden appearance of an enormous variety of fossilized marine creatures.

In keeping with the theme of this episode, there are two teams that will discuss the evidence found at this site. The evolutionary team is called the Explorer's Society and is represented by the fossil animal known as the trilobite. The creation team is called Creation Response Team and is represented by the fossil animal known as the Marrella. We will encounter both of these fossil animals in the Burgess Shale of Walcott Quarry.

Formation of the Layers

The Explorers' Society

Creation Response Team

The Explorers' Society says that the Cambrian layers of rock are around 500 million years old. They believe each layer was laid down a while after the one below it - and each represents a different age. The fossils found in each of the layers are the creatures that were alive during that time.

They say this site is important because it shows how life suddenly evolved into many different forms. They claim that the animals found in the first rock layer evolved into the animals found the layers above it.

The Creation Response Team says that the Cambrian layers of rocks were deposited during the world-wide flood. They believe that each layer represents a rapidly deposited layer made close to the same time, not over millions of years. The creatures found in the Precambrian layers were alive at the same time as those found in the Cambrian layer.

The Point is that there are two basic ways to look at the rock layers: Short amount of time and a long amount of time.

How did the Burgess Shale layer form?

Amazingly both teams agree... and disagree ...

Agreement

Underwater landslides instantly swept and buried the animals with powerful surges of water.

Disagreement

They disagree on an important point: TIME!

The Explorers' Society

They believe there were several catastrophic events over a very long period of time. They claim this area formed over 5-10 million years by periodic underwater landslides. They believe animals lived there during this long period of time, and that each time a landslide happened, it caught some of the creatures at their current point in evolution and buried and fossilized them. Others survived and were caught in later landslides. For this reason, they believe that these layers are a record of the continuous evolution that was happening there.

Creation Response Team

The Creation Response Team says that there is good evidence that one catastrophic event deposited the layers very quickly. They believe there were waves of underwater sediment gravity flows, and that the layers were deposited one right after another. Each underwater landslide picked up more of the animals and rapidly deposited them, causing swift fossilization. Since it all happened quickly, they believe all the different types of animals fossilized in the layers were living at the same time.

So who is right? Was it a long period of time, or a short one?

Proofs of Rapid Burial:

Proof #1: The Molting Marrella

Marrella splendens is one creature found at the site. Molting is how they grow by shedding their skin, or exoskeleton, and exposing a new layer below. Incredibly, they discovered a Marrella that was fossilized in the process of molting. This is amazing because molting only takes a few minutes so it would have been buried instantly.

Proof #2: Amazing preservation of soft parts

Think of the body of a jellyfish. Its entire body is soft. Muscle and skin are also soft body parts. A jellyfish has no shell or bones that are considered hard body parts. Bones and shells fossilize much better than soft parts because soft parts are very fragile.

In order for soft parts to become fossilized there must be special conditions: Split second burial by sediment and water.

And yet there are many other types of soft-bodied animals that have been fossilized at Walcott Quarry! This fits well with the idea that these creatures were buried rapidly!

Round #1: How much time did it take to form the layers at Walcott Quarry?
Evidence best fits the Creation Response Team's position.

Explosion of Life

The Explorers' Society

Creation Response Team

According to the Explorers' Society the Precambrian layer (the layer just below the Cambrian) shows the first few animals to evolve.

The next layer up, the Cambrian shows an explosion of many new animals that evolved from the fossils found in the Precambrian layer.

They claim that there was lots of room for new creatures to live in because there was not much competition from other animals since there were not many around at that time. The environment was ready for a burst of life. They believe that these new types of creatures evolved by mutations - or accidental mistakes in their genetic code. There was 5-10 million years available for the new animals to evolve from the Precambrian animals into the ones seen in the Cambrian layer.

The Creation Response Team believes that during this time that all the created kinds already existed. It just so happens that the animals that are fossilized at the Walcott Quarry are the ones that were caught and deposited there by the worldwide flood.

Here snapshots of three creatures found in the Walcott layers.

There are around 35 different types of marine phyla found in the Burgess shale.

There is the Tuzoia-a crustacean similar to brine shrimp.

The Marrella splendens is one of the most common creatures in the Burgess shale. It is a type of arthropod.

There is the trilobite which is also common in the shale.

Because the organisms found in these layers are so different and unique, they are examined and placed into groups using the classification system.

Classification

There are about 43 total known marine phyla, and 35 of them are found in the Burgess shale. Do you know what a phylum is? It is part of the classification system that scientists use to give names to creatures. Phyla represent the general body plan of the creature.

Remember the seven layers of the classification system? The top layer is a broad category and as you move down it becomes more specific.

Kingdom
Phylum
Class
Order
Family
Genus
Species

Here is an example: Read the items in the box starting at the bottom.

Classification of the Lion

Kingdom: Animalia (animal)
Phylum (body type): Chordata (symmetrical, elongated structure)
Class: Mammalia (mammal)
Order: Carnivora (carnivore)
Family: Felidae (cats)
Genus: Panthera (all great roaring cats)
Species: Leo (lion)

Classification is tricky business. Animals that lack backbones are known as invertebrates. They belong to a subphylum (or subcategory under phylum) called invertebrata. Over 98% of species on earth are invertebrates. Some invertebrate phyla have only one species while others like Arthropoda (animals with jointed feet such as crustaceans, insects, millipedes and centipedes) include more than 800,000 species.

Top of the Class Game

Draw a square around the animals that have a back bone.
Draw a circle around the animals that have an exoskeleton.
Draw a triangle around the animals that have live births.
Draw a rectangle around the animals that lay eggs.
Underline the animals that have many jointed appendages.
Put a star by the animals that have fused body segments (body parts that are connected).

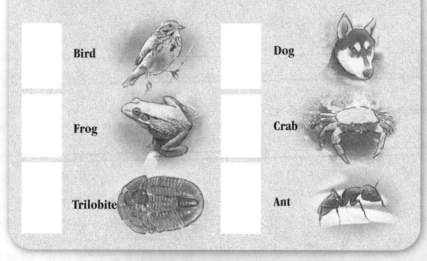

Bird

Dog

Frog

Crab

Trilobite

Ant

That is what makes classifying animals so hard, animals can be grouped completely differently, depending on which traits you use! Evolutionists are trying to group animals based on similarities because they believe that alike animals most likely evolved from common ancestors. But for a creationist, we realize that animals are just similar in some ways because they were made by the same Creator. That also explains why completely different animals can have similar traits as some, and completely different similarities to others (just like in the "Top of the Class Game").

Genesis 1:24 *"And God said, Let the earth bring forth the living creature after his kind, cattle, and creeping thing, and beast of the earth after his kind: and it was so."*

Some of the creatures that God created are found in the Burgess Shale and forever saved for us to see the great variety in creation. Below is a diagram of two of these rock layers where we find this variety. Observe the diagram below:

Trilobites   Arthropods

Marrella   Anomalocaris   Corals

Tuzoia   **Cambrian**   Worms

Echinoderi   Clams   Jellies

Brachiopods   Natiloid   Waptia

Worms   Sponges

Precambrian

Bacteria   Jellies

What is the name of the bottom rock layer that we've been talking about?

What is the name of the next rock layer on top of it?

How many animals can you find in each layer?

What evidence can you observe from the drawing?

_____

_____

_____

_____

Your observations may include these:
-There are only 4 types of animals in the lower layer.
-There are many types of animals in the next layer on top.

What is the meaning of the sudden appearance of so many animals in these layers?

If evolution were true, then there should be evolutionary grandparents of the jellies, worms, and sponges in the Precambrian, but there aren't any! All we see is fully formed worms and sponges - and no ancestors to the other animals found in the Cambrian.

However, there is even another problem in the Precambrian as well. The animals found in the first rock layer have no evolutionary ancestors either!

To explain why we do not find evolutionary ancestors in the Precambrian layer, evolutionists say that these animals would have had soft-bodies, and that they probably would not have fossilized. However, this is not true because we have found tons of fossilized animals with soft bodies. So the problem remains. Why are we missing the evolutionary ancestors if evolution is true?

The Arthropods

You met three arthropods earlier in the lesson the trilobite, marrella, and tuozia. Can you tell what three things these animals have in common?

All arthropods have a skeleton on the outside of their bodies called an exoskeleton. Could you imagine what we would look like with our skeletons on the outside? Weird.

In insects the three segments are joined forming the head, thorax, and abdomen.

Head   **Thorax**   **Abdomen**

Arthropods also have joined or modified segments.

Arthropods also have many jointed appendages like arms or legs.

Arthropoda is the largest phylum and is composed of insects, crustaceans (including shellfish), and arachnids (spiders). Nearly 4/5 of all living animals are arthropods.

Arthropods are abundant in the seas and oceans of the world and we see this abundance captured in the fossils of the burgess shale.

The Creation Response Team Argument: There are no Grandmothers or Grandfathers

Creation Response Team

The arthropod is the most common type of fossil in the Burgess shale. We have many arthropods living today and the first time that they appear in the fossil record they are distinctly arthropods. There are no transitional creatures becoming arthropods.

So who is right? How do explain the sudden explosion of life?

Proofs that these Fossils Were Created Kinds Caught in the Flood:

Proof #1: Mutations

Mutations have never been observed to create new, functional structures in an animal. Therefore it is impossible that these mutations could explain one animal evolve into another.

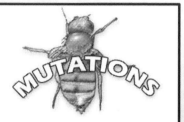

Proof #2: Time

If the evolutionary story was true, then there would have to be a huge amount of evolution happening in a very short time (5-10 million years is very quick from an evolutionary perspective). Even if mutations could make new animals (which has never been observed) 5-10 million years is much too short to fit with evolutionary rates of mutation.

Proof #3: No ancestors

Rapid burial of the fossils, fossilized soft bodied animals, lack of transitional organisms, and the variety of arthropods support the theory that God created these animals already fully formed.

Round #2: Sudden Explosion of Life
Evidence best fits the Creation Response Team's position.

Persistent Morphological Isolation

The Explorers Society claims there was a continuous evolution as the animals in the Precambrian turned into the animals we see in the Cambrian Explosion. Since that time, those animals have continued to evolve into the animals that we have today.

The Creation Response Team believes that Persistent Morphological Isolation shows the evolutionary claim to be wrong.

What is the Creation Response Team talking about? What is Persistent Morphological Isolation? Let's take each one of those words and learn what they mean...

Morphological

Morphology- the study of the form and structure of an animal.

Scientists are interested in the body plans of the animals at the Burgess shale.

Here are two types of body plans:

Radial symmetry

Animals that have radial symmetry have body parts arranged equally around a central disc, like spokes of a bike wheel. If you were to cut it in half the first cut divides it into equal halves, second cut divides into equal quarters and so on.
Example: Sea Anemone

Bi-lateral symmetry

Animals that have bi-lateral symmetry have a right half and left half. If you were to cut it in half each side would be mirror images of each other.
Example: Creyfish

Three More Amazing Creatures

NEWS FLASH

This amazing thing is actually a claw of a ferocious fossil creature!

Anomalocaris

Waptia

Waptia is a crustacean which is an arthropod that Scientists think lived on the bottom of the ocean walking on its jointed legs searching for food in the sediment. It was usually about 3 inches long.

Eldoniaoida

Activity

"What is this thing?"

The 'thing' is called Hallucigenia.

Is it a plant or an animal? _____

Do you think it lived on the land or in the sea? _____

Is this the whole plant or animal or some of it? _____

Which end is up? _____

If it is an animal label the body parts (i.e. head, tail, legs, arms)

How do you think it moved? _____

What did it eat? _____

If it is a plant, how big do you think it was? _____

Does it have a stem, roots, or top? _____

Describe how it lived? _____

Draw what you think
this fossil looks like by
examining the pictures
of the fossil.

Did you find that drawing it was easy or hard?

How might scientists find it hard to see what a fossil animal actually looks like and what phylum to place it into?

There are some wild fossil creatures! Have you noticed how different they all look? Their form and structure is known as their morphology.

Isolation

Do you know what it means to feel alone or be by yourself? The word isolation means just that.

Look at the pictures. They all have completely different morphology. In other words, they all look so differently on the outside that you'd never say that a ball became a car or a shoe - or visa versa. They are completely separate from each other. In other words their morphology (their form and structure) are so different they are completely isolated from one another.

The animals found in the Burgess shale have body plans that are isolated from each other, in the sense of being one of a kind. They look like no other creature so their body design separates them from each other.

Persistent

Often you hear this term in relation to people being persistent like the widow talked about in Luke 18. She knocked and knocked again until finally someone answered and helped her with her need. This is being persistent. Being persistent means to continue, without stopping.

When we apply this to the fossils we see at the Burgess Shale, it means that not only are the animals completely different from each other, but they persist to be different. In other words, through the rest of the fossil record, they continue to stay separate.

Persistent Morphological Isolation

Now that we've looked at each word in this phrase, we can understand what it means:
It means that the body shapes of the animals are completely different from each other and continue to be through the whole fossil record.

Proof: Persistent Morphological Isolation

When we observe the fossils at the Walcott Quarry, we do not see any fossils that are half of one type of animal and half of another. The animals are completely different from one another. Further, we see that these differences continue in the fossil record.

Round 3

There does not seem to be evidence of evolution in the Precambrian or the Cambrian layers.
Evidence best fits the Creation Response Team's position.

The Evolutionary Tree

Gradual evolution is often pictured as a diagram called the evolutionary tree. The tree is supposed to show you the path of evolution from a simple cell to a complex human.

Evolutionary Tree

The Explorers' Society

Darwin is known to have brought out the idea that life started as a single cell and as time passes this cell has evolved into more and more complex organisms. Evolution assumes that similarities between organisms mean they have a common ancestor.

The tree diagram tries to show that the single cell is at the bottom. Then the next organisms that evolve are placed a little farther up the tree because they are similar to the first cell. As you climb up the tree the organisms get more and more different and farther and farther away from the original cell at the bottom. In other words, organisms should be very similar at the bottom of the tree, and become more and more different as you go up the tree.

Creation Response Team

The Creation Response Team says that exactly the opposite is true. Instead of animals starting off being very similar (as they evolve from a common ancestor), they would start off very distinct from one another since God created them as different kinds. Over time, each individual kind of animal would begin to express the variety that God programmed into them. So instead of one evolutionary tree in which a single cell branched out into all life, creationists believe in a graph that would look like an orchard. Each tree in the orchard represents a single kind created by God. One tree can never become another tree, and yet each tree branches out as that kind of animal expresses it's own variety.

45

Proof #1: Fossils at the Burgess Shale are different

The fossils at the Walcott Quarry show many different animals that are not very similar. Yet if evolution were true, it seems that since these fossils supposedly come from the bottom of the evolutionary tree they should be very similar since they are coming from a common ancestor. Like we've mentioned before, the animals there represent about 35 phyla, which are broad categories of animals. That means that these animals are not similar, but very different toward the bottom of the fossil record.

Proof #2: Animals found at the Burgess Shale are seen with variation later

We do see some of the same animals from the Burgess Shale either alive today, or from another spot in the fossil record. They are still the same kind of animal, but have expressed different variations.

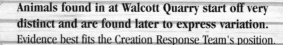

Animals found in at Walcott Quarry start off very distinct and are found later to express variation. Evidence best fits the Creation Response Team's position.

NEWS FLASH

Ladies and Gentlemen that concludes the battle between the Explorers' Society and the Creation Response Team. And the Creation Response Team wins! There was a lot of complicated information being talked about.

Let's see if we can make a short summary.

The Cambrian explosion shows a huge variety of fossilized life.

We have seen snapshots of a few of these creatures.

All these fossils show the marine life that God created and was buried during the world wide flood.

We observe:

Split second burial of soft bodied animals and a molting arthropod

Huge variety of marine animal fossils

No evolutionary grandmothers or grandfathers

Persistent Morphological Isolation

Distinct kinds expressing variation

Creation has a lot to tell us about God and ourselves.

In the Bible, Job 12:7-9 says *"But ask now the beasts, and they shall teach thee; and the fowls of the air, and they shall tell thee: ⁸Or speak to the earth, and it shall teach thee: and the fishes of the sea shall declare unto thee. ⁹Who knoweth not in all these that the hand of the LORD hath wrought this?"*

So we look to a particular mountain called Mount St. Helens in this episode and ask what it can tell us about God and about our world.

'Well since you are asking, I, Miss Mount St. Helens, will tell you how I show God's power.'

Mount St. Helens is located in the Cascade Range, which stretches from British Columbia, Canada to California.

WA

Raineer
Adams
Mount St. Helens
Hood
Jefferson

OR

'I got my name from an explorer who sailed up the Columbia River, Capt. Peter Vancouver who named me after a friend, the Baron Saint Helens.'

The first place we can see God's power through Mount St. Helens is in an earthquake that took place in 1980!

It all started at 8:32am on May 18th ...

Today Is

18

121   244

Sunday
May   1980

49

On a quiet Sunday morning, western Washington residents were suddenly startled by a 5.1 magnitude earthquake. Next, was a landslide of 3.3 billion cubic yards from the top and insides of the mountain that fell into the valley below. It created the largest landslide caught on film!

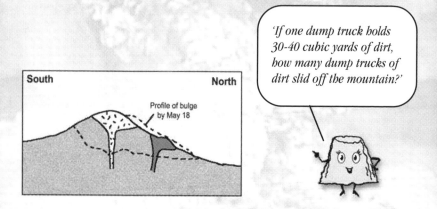

'If one dump truck holds 30-40 cubic yards of dirt, how many dump trucks of dirt slid off the mountain?'

The second place we see God's power in Mount St. Helens is in the explosion!

As the landslide moved down the side of the mountain, the volcanic pressure that had been building under the surface was released. In 30 seconds, the explosion

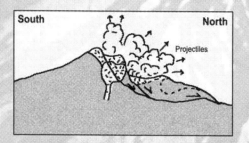

burst out at full strength and throughout the next three minutes it tore down the side of the mountain and through the surrounding forest, killing 57 people and flattening 230 square miles up to 17 miles away.

And this brings us to the third way we see God's power through Mount St. Helens. In it's ERUPTION!

What followed the blast was nine hours of vertical eruption with 30 times the energy of the sideways blast, sending ash 60,000 feet into the sky and throwing out about 30 feet of ash on top of the landslide deposit.

This landslide and the sideways blasts are important because it points out how fast the earth can change through a catastrophic event. This eruption also tells us about how the earth came to look like what it does today.

In 3 1/2 minutes the mountain was clearly changed - the top was gone, the middle was hollowed out into an open crater, and 234 square miles of forest were destroyed.

This all helps us to better understand the worldwide flood that raged for a year and shaped and reshaped every square mile of the earth's surface over and over.

So what's the BIG DEAL about this volcano?

Why is the explosion at Mount St. Helens so important? Because it provides a lot of evidence that supports the creation theory, and particularly the ideas of a young earth and the worldwide flood.

Let's take a look at 4 different evidences from the eruption of Mount St. Helens that support the creation theory for the rapid catastrophic formation of the earth as we see it today. The key to all of the evidence talked about here is the word "rapid." Be sure to notice how many times we use this word! Things that happen rapidly, shorten the amount of time needed for the earth's surface to change.

1. Rapid Layering

If you visited Mount St. Helens today, you would be able to see both really thin and really thick layers of dirt. Each layer is different, both in color and texture, because the contents of each are different. These are called sediment, and all this variation is the result of Rapid Layering. When Mount St. Helens erupted, it created both very small and very large layers of sediment in only one day, something once thought to be impossible by evolutionists. Let's find out how this happened!

How could this happen?

First the landslide covered the area with a huge amount of material.

Then the pyroclastic flows put another 25 feet of sediment on top.

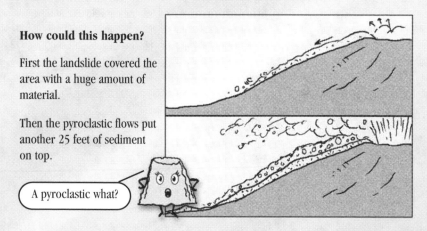

A pyroclastic what?

A pyroclastic flow is a high-density mixture of broken rocks, pumice, ash, and hot gases that move away from the vent at high speeds.

After these materials where blown 45,000 feet into the air they began to fall back to the ground. As the gas disappeared into the air, the other material began skipping along the ground, sorting itself as it formed layer after layer. Some layers are ultra-thin and some are three feet thick. Scientists have counted about 200 distinct layers.

Why is this important?
Because it was once thought that it took many many years to make layers like the ones that we see at this mountain. But, in fact we see some that were made in one day!

2. Rapid Carving of Canyons

Along with the many layers created by the explosion and eruption of the mountain, there were also many canyons carved by this catastrophe, some in one day and others over several months. Two such examples are Step Canyon and Loowit Canyon. Both were carved out of 100 feet of solid rock over a period of a few months following the eruption. Creeks now flow through each and Step Canyon is over 700 feet deep in some places!

Why is this important?
Creationists use this evidence to support the idea that the rapid processes at Mount St. Helens can be compared to those that may have carved other canyons rapidly, such as the Grand Canyon. In the past, the Grand Canyon was thought to have been carved by river erosion over millions of years. However, because of such examples as Step and Loowit canyons, some scientists are beginning to rethink that timetable!

3. Rapid Recovery

Just like the explosion rapidly carved canyons and stripped the land of trees, animals, soil, and other plants, just as rapidly has been the return of these things back to the land!

Only 20 years after the eruption how have things recovered? This picture illustrates the things that began to happen.

What kinds of things can you observe from the drawing? Possible observations:

The old plants were coming back
New plants coming in through birds and other animals
Gophers never left they just dug in and came out when it was over
Fish are reappearing
Tailed frogs appeared
Elk came back

The return of the Elk is particularly interesting. Usually Elk have one baby every two or three years. At that rate it would take a l-o-n-g time to rebuild their population. However, a curious thing happened after the eruption. As soon as the elk moved back into the area, they started having twins or triplets every year! And even though there were no longer any tall trees to provide the shade they needed to stay cool, they changed their normal behavior and cool off by burying themselves in the mud!

This ability to adapt to changes in their surroundings could be the same God-given mechanism that allowed all the animals to rapidly re-populate the earth after Noah's flood.

Why is this important?
It was once thought that it could take over 100 years for the area around the mountain to recover, but in only 20 years life was flourishing once again. This supports the theory that the plants and animals could have multiplied and spread out quickly after the worldwide flood.

4. Rapid Deposit of Logs

The fourth piece of evidence supporting the creation theory is something that we observed after the dust settled from the Mount St. Helens eruption.

Millions of trees were uprooted and knocked over like a forest of toothpicks during the eruption. Many of the logs were left to float in a huge log mat in Spirit Lake. Slowly they became soaked with water and began to sink to the bottom, some in a standing position because the root end got water-logged first and dragged the tree down upright. About 20% of the trees that sunk landed upright.

Then, as the sediment continued to fall into the lake, it buried the bottoms of the standing logs, making them look like they were planted in that spot.

This would look like an actual forest if it were above the water!

Also, different types of trees sank faster than others. Silver and Noble firs sank before Douglas Firs, creating different layers of forest on top of each other.

In Yellowstone National Park, there is a petrified forest having over 27 different layers. The layers are like those at Mount St. Helens with a sediment layer, trees, more sediment and then more trees. At Yellowstone, they are interpreted to mean that there were 27 different forests growing at different times in history over millions of years. Hey, but doesn't that layering sound familiar?

These are the things that you can observe at Yellowstone: the whole deposit was made by something fast and strong. Half of the fossil trees at Yellowstone are standing upright and appear to have actual soil sediment around their bases. None of the trees have a complete root system as they would if they grew in the place where they now stand.

Get a set of play blocks. Imagine that the floor is the bottom of the lake. Place three tall square rectangular blocks standing upright onto the carpet layer. This represents the trees that have sunk to the bottom of the lake. Then lay flat rectangular blocks that fit snugly around the bases of the "trees," making a continuous layer. (See diagram.) This represents a sediment layer that has sunk to the bottom of the lake. Now place three more trees on top of this layer, which represents a new set of trees that have sunk to the bottom. Now place another layer of flat rectangular blocks around the trees. Depending on how many blocks you have you can make several layers in this manner.

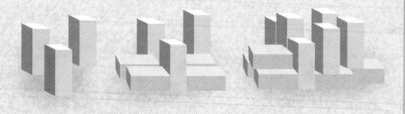

Through this illustration, you can imagine the sediment layers, tree layers, and different heights of the trees as they would be at the bottom of Spirit Lake.

Why is this important?

Until the recent example of the sinking logs in Spirit Lake, evolutionists claimed that other similar examples were the result of millions of years of growth. The rapid deposit of logs at the bottom of Spirit Lake provided more evidence to support creationism, the flood of Noah, and the young earth concept!

Most evolutionists deny the creationist interpretation of Yellowstone, but take a look at the evidence presented. What do you think?

Evolutionists' Arguments Against the Creationists Claims:

1) Many of the fossil trees at Yellowstone have been buried in sediments that come from high-energy flows, not a calm lake like Spirit Lake.

2) While 50% of the trees are found upright at Yellowstone, only 20% were deposited upright at Spirit Lake.

3) Actual soil sediment have been found around the trees indicating that they grew there.

Creationist Response:

1) The high energy flows (fast and strong) suggests a large catastrophe.

2) Yellowstone and Mount St. Helens are two different sites, so the number of upright trees is irrelevant.

3) Soil was probably transported into place at Yellowstone just like what we can see at Mount St. Helens. So it doesn't have to mean the trees grew there. Further, the trees at Yellowstone don't have the root systems like we'd expect if they had grown in place there.

Don't be Petrified!

When you visit Yellowstone National Park you will find this petrified forest explained in the traditional evolutionary manner, but what if it is ALL wrong? The evidence found at Mount St. Helens suggests that the Yellowstone petrified forest may not be a petrified forest, trees that grew were they are now found, but rather the aftermath of a much larger catastrophe that happened in the past.

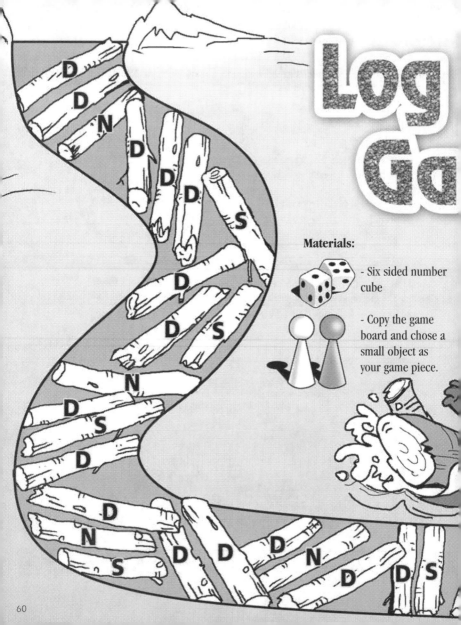

Log Game

Materials:

- Six sided number cube

- Copy the game board and chose a small object as your game piece.

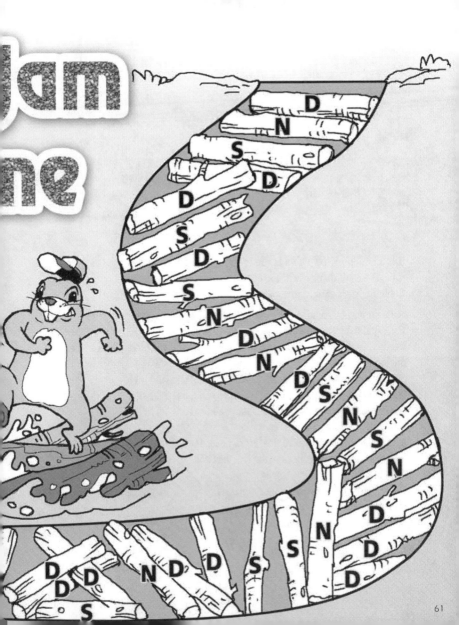

A river has been clogged by a log jam. Pretend that you are a gofer and have been stranded on one end of the river and need to get to the other end where the food is. Roll the number cube and jump the corresponding number of logs. Each log has a letter on it:

Douglas   **Spruce**   **Noble**

If you land on a log with a D you are safe. If you land on a S or N, the log will sink. You have three free lives, but the fourth time that you land on a Silver or Noble log your game is over. One to four people can play at a time.

1. Begin play by rolling to see who goes first - highest roller starts.

2. Start at the left top of the game board. Going clockwise, each of the players rolls the dice, and moves their game token the same number of logs to get to the end of the log jam.

3. Each player starts off with 3 "lives". Each time you land on a "sinking log" (a (S)pruce or (N)obel log) you loose a life. If a player looses all three "lives", then they sink and are out of the game!

4. If a player roles a 3, then they get to go again. If there first roll landed them on a sinking log, they don't loose a life.

5. If a player roles a 6, then after moving 6 logs ahead, they can then move any other player to the next sinking log. The other player losses a "life".

6. To win, a player must be the first one to reach the end of the log jam!

5. Dating a Lava Dome Rock

Scientists test to see how old volcanic rocks are by using a method called radioisotope dating. There are certain types of rocks that contain a radio active material, such as potassium. This potassium slowly turns into argon. To find the age of the rock, they measure how much potassium and how much argon is left.

The Three Assumptions

1. That we know how much potassium and argon there was to begin with
2. That the rate potassium decays into argon stays the same.
3. That there has been no contamination in the rock sample.

Remember that if the assumptions are false, the dating method will give false ages. So how do you know the assumptions are right? By doing an experiment.

Dr. Steve Austin did just that. He did an experiment to test assumption #1.

Setting up the experiment:

First he had to find a 'new-born' rock, one that had just come out of a mountain in the form of hot lava like in the dome at Mount St. Helens. This would test assumption #1 because at the time the rock was less than 15 years old.

A new-born rock is one that was liquid rock coming up from beneath the earth's crust that has hardened.

If the dating method works it would confirm our known age of less than 15 years.

Next he sent it to a lab to find the amount of potassium and argon in the rock. As the potassium in the rock gets older it breaks down into argon, so the lab will measure the amount of argon and potassium in the rock, and we can work backward to find the age of the rock.

If the dating method works there should be little or NO argon in the rock, thus giving us a very young age.

The lab sent back a range of numbers and then the scientists interpreted the numbers to find an approximate age for the rock.

The range of numbers that Dr. Steve Austin got back for his rock gave dates from 350,000 years to 2.4 million years old.

= 350,000 – 2.4 million years old

By looking at the range of ages for the rock, can you tell if this is *in favor of* or *against* assumption #1 being true?

Conclusions: The results of this experiment suggest that the dating method using radioisotopes is very wrong, misleading, and confusing.

How can a rock of known age of about 15 years be tested with results of 350,000 - 2.4 million years? Only if something is wrong with the method for dating rocks.

Evolution's Objections to Our Conclusions

Scientists who rely on these dating methods would disagree with our conclusions in two ways:

-The lab the rock sample was sent to was not a lab that had tools sensitive enough to measure the small amount of argon that would be present in a young-aged rock. This would result in misleading numbers.

- The next argument would be that Dr. Steve Austin did not remove any parts of the sample that were older than the young rock. This would yield an old age instead of a young age.

"Oh my do I really look that old?"

Creation Rebuttal

Creationists would agree that you need sensitive tools for accurate measurements but would also point out that one of the measurements that was reported (2.4 million) is in the range of the labs measurable parameters.

It is known that Dr. Austin's sample was as clean and was not contaminated.

Why is this important?

There are problems with the methods used to date rocks. Through an experiment, it appears that one of the key assumptions of the method is false. This means that the ages of rocks given by scientists may all be wrong; the rocks of the earth may be much younger than the reported ages!!!! This supports the creation theory.

Hopefully you noticed how often the word 'rapid' was used in this episode. Mount St. Helens is exceptional evidence that shows how quickly formations of the earth can be made. It does not take thousands of years to carve a canyon or re-inhabit a devastated area. God has designed the processes of nature to rapidly rejuvenate to ensure life to the generations of creatures that He created.

We discussed:

Rapid layering
Rapid carving
Rapid recovery
Rapid deposition of logs
Methods of dating rocks

Can you remember something about each thing we talked about?

Choose something in nature that you are interested in and ask it to tell you something about itself and God as the scripture in Job states. God can reveal himself to you through creation. Write the things that you learn down in a journal.

Have you ever heard of Ellesmere Island? Probably not! It is an island near the North Pole in the Canadian arctic just to the west of Greenland. Only about 200 people live on the whole island, most in the settlement of Grise Fiord. The number of people living on the island drops in the coldest months, many of them in the settlement of Alert, the most Northern "city" in the world.

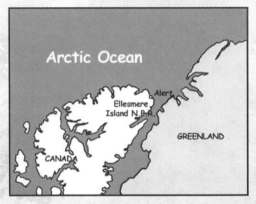

With temperatures from -40°C in the winter to only 20°C in the short "summer" months, continuous sunlight or darkness that goes on for months depending on the season, and a continual ice pack on the nearby Arctic Ocean, the term "rugged" is a bit of an understatement for this part of the planet! These are just a few of the reasons why scientists have found fossil research and exploration there to be a challenge.

However, scientists have discovered some unusual fossils in the area. One of these finds has become known as Tiktaalik rosea. It is a fish that has tetrapod (Latin for four-legged)-like characteristics and evolutionists claim that it fills the gap of transitional fossils between fish and land animals. Let's learn more about it ...

What is a Tetrapod?

Technically, a tetrapod is an animal that has a back bone and four limbs.

"Okay," you say. "That could mean just about any animal!"

You're right! However, the term usually refers to more salamander-type amphibians. That narrows the field quite a bit!

Evolutionists believe that tetrapods were the earliest limbed animals.

A first look at Tiktaalik

This fossil fish is what evolutionists call a "transitional fossil," or one that shows how one animal evolved into another. It was found in 2004 on Ellesmere Island in rock from the Devonian period, supposedly making it about about 375 million years old, and had characteristics of two different types of animals.

Here are some of the characteristics that make it so interesting:

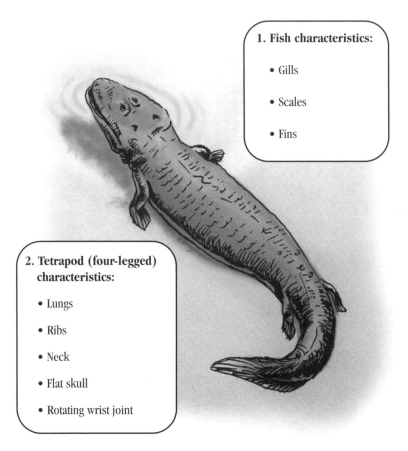

1. Fish characteristics:

- Gills

- Scales

- Fins

2. Tetrapod (four-legged) characteristics:

- Lungs

- Ribs

- Neck

- Flat skull

- Rotating wrist joint

So what does that all mean? First of all, there is no mistaking it as a fish. So the next questions we need to answer is what type of fish it is and is it really an example of evolution?

Classification of Fish

There are so many types of fish that scientists have put them into groups.

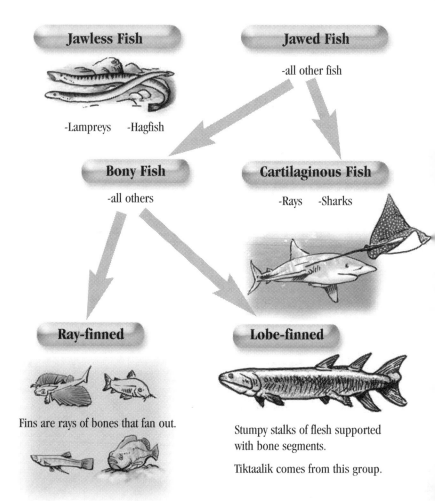

Jawless Fish

-Lampreys   -Hagfish

Jawed Fish

-all other fish

Bony Fish

-all others

Cartilaginous Fish

-Rays   -Sharks

Ray-finned

Fins are rays of bones that fan out.

Lobe-finned

Stumpy stalks of flesh supported with bone segments.

Tiktaalik comes from this group.

Evolutionists look at this diagram to find common traits as a sign that all fish have one common ancestor that they evolved from.

The common traits are things like scales, gills, fins, and egg laying ...

can you think of others?

**AAHHH
I Don't Get It!**

Creationists would say that many fish *are* similar but not ALL fish have a common ancestor. Instead, there may have been one or more original created kind of bony fish that lead to all the other various types of bony fish we see today. There also may have been an original created kind of cartilaginous fish that has given rise to all of the other cartilaginous types we see today.

Do you have a friend who looks like you? Have people confused you for being brothers or sisters? Just because you look the same does not mean that you are related. For a creationist, just because some animals have the same characteristics, does not mean they are related.

A bat and a bird both have wings so that they can fly but a bat is a mammal and a bird is a bird. They are not related even though they both need wings because of the lifestyle and niche that they were created to fill.

In other words, the presence and function of the wings is not a common ancestral link, but an important design for their individual habitats.

"And God said, Let the waters bring forth abundantly the moving creature that hath life, and fowl that may fly above the earth in the open firmament of heaven. And God created great whales, and every living creature that moveth, which the waters brought forth abundantly, after their kind, and every winged fowl after his kind: and God saw that it was good." - Genesis 1:20-21

Again, creationists look at the previous diagram and see an original created kind as Genesis 1:20-21 talks about; each kind reproducing after itself.

So To Summarize ...

Evolutionists and creationists look at animals differently because they start with different assumptions. Evolutionists assume all things are related through a line of descent. Creationists assume that animals are designed with traits that help them live in their special habitat. Each Biblical 'kind' would have been created by God and then adapted to its special habitat through the generations. This is not evolution because God already pre-programmed this genetic ability into the original kinds from the very beginning.

A creationist would predict that we would find different creatures that have similar traits, even thought they are not related, because they need the same function to live in their habitat. Creatures that have several of these types of traits are often called "mosaics."

Mosaic Creatures

Mosaic works of art are composed of many little pieces that make up a whole picture.

A mosaic creature is an animal that has characteristics that match one or more different animals, such as the Platypus.

The Platypus's Mosaic Characteristics:
- It is a mammal that lays eggs like a reptile
- It has a bill and webbed feet like a duck
- It has a tail like a beaver
- It has spurs on its hind feet (like a spiny anteater) with venom!

**AAHHH
I Don't Get It!**

The eye of a squid and the eye of a human are called convergent traits. The eyes are very similar but no one claims that squid are related to humans. These traits are evidence for design!!!

Where could this animal get all these characteristics?

Evolution explains away this amazing animal by using the term "convergence." This means that sometimes they see the same traits on animals that are obviously not related. They just call it a *convergent trait*. They believe that these similar traits simply evolved two different times. For more information about supposed convergent evolution, see the chapter titled, *Mysterious Stranger* in the Album #2 Study Guide.

The platypus is a mosaic animal that has characteristics similar to several different animals.

Just like the Platypus is a mosaic animal, Tiktaalik may be a mosaic fish.

Let's look at its tetrapod qualities: (remember, a tetrapod is an animal with a backbone and four limbs)

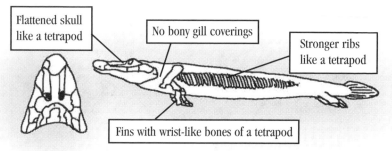

Flattened skull like a tetrapod

No bony gill coverings

Stronger ribs like a tetrapod

Fins with wrist-like bones of a tetrapod

Remember that this is a fossil fish so it is unknown as to how it actually lived in its habitat. We do not know if it 'walked' or supported itself with its fins as scientists speculate. Scientists assumed the same thing about a fossil fish called the coelacanth, but when a few live specimens were found in 1938, they discovered that it did not use its lobed fins to 'walk' or prop itself up in the shallow bottom of a river as they had thought!

Did you know that there are several types of fish that can do something similar to walking? These animals can wiggle on the shore and spend hours out of the water.

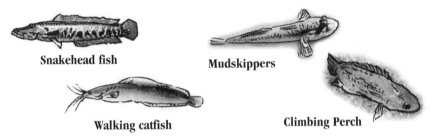

Snakehead fish

Mudskippers

Walking catfish

Climbing Perch

Evolutionists however do not put these fish in the evolutionary line of tetrapods because they have no other common traits.

These fish are actually strong evidence that each kind of animal is made with characteristics that enable it to survive in the habitat that God designed it for.

The Tiktaalik is evidence that also supports design.

The special shape of its head, bones in its arm, strong ribs, and no gill cover appear to make the fish well suited for its special environment.

A Little Summary

Mosaic animals are unique with traits that are similar to traits that are seen in different types of animals, which help them to survive in their special habitat. Tiktaalik may have been such an animal. This just means that these traits were already built into the DNA of the fish and when it became isolated in its special habitat these traits were expressed.

Since God first created the world, all the needed information for different animals to survive was already present within the animal, and a creature's ability to adapt to its environment does not take very long.

Evolution's Problem of Time

According to evolution, there is a span of 20 million years between the fossil layers of Tiktaalik and the first tetrapod that walked on land.

For evolution, 20 million years is a short amount of time. In this time, the fish had to become a land walking, air breathing animal.

The large gap between a fish and a tetrapod is large. Even if mutations could turn one animal into another (which they can't) it would take far too much new information to change the fish into an amphibian. Mutations could never do this -- even in the 20 million year timetable.

**AAHHH
I Don't Get It!**

The way a change supposedly happens in evolution is by mutations. Mutations are tiny mistakes in a creature's DNA. Generations of the same type of creature would need millions of good mistakes to change a structure such as a fin into a foot. Even 20 million years is not enough time for this to happen. As a matter of fact, mutations are so overwhelmingly bad, that the more time that passes, the worse off the creature would become.

Here is a picture of a fish and a salamander. Make a list of the types of changes that the fish would have to go through in order to become a salamander. Remember to write down things that you cannot see from a picture (such as lungs or gills).

The first tetrapod fossils look similar to salamanders. Salamanders that are alive today have changed little from their fossil relatives. If the changes from fish to salamander did happen in 20 million years, then why have there been no changes in salamanders since that time? How could they suddenly evolve and then stop evolving for over 160 million years of evolutionary time?

A Summary

Evolutionists say that there is enough time for mutations to bring about the needed changes in a fish for it to become a land animal. However the evidence shows that mutations cannot even turn one type of animal into another. It seems like 20 million years is a long time¡Kand it is in terms of the Bible, but for an evolutionist it is only 1/225,000,000 of their timetable! Yet, their millions of years work against them because mutations actually destroy a creature instead of making it better.

Color the mosaic.

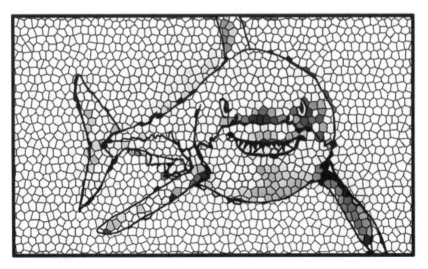

The Fin 'Progression'

Let's talk about what exactly makes this unique fossil a transitional species for an evolutionist. There are several traits that they point towards as proof. One of these proofs is the lobed-fin that is supposedly 'becoming' a foot.

The Claim: The fin bone segments of Tiktaalik look like the beginning of a wrist and toes.

The Requirements: In order for something to be a TRUE evolutionary sequence it must meet three requirements.

1. **Morphologic sequence** - This means that the fin must show a progression of change in structure from fin to foot.

This is an example of a progression from 2 to 5 shapes

'Youngest' Rock Layer

2. **Geologic sequence** - This means that the fossils must be found in sequence in the correct rock layers.

This is an example of a progression with in layers. Notice that as you go up in the sequence from 1-4 the number of shapes also smoothly increases

4	
3	
2	
1	

'Oldest' Rock Layer

3. **Adaptive value** - This means that the changes must help the creature to fit its environment better.

Let's look more closely at each one of these requirements as it applies to Tiktaalik, starting with change in structure (called morphology).

Morphological sequence:

Fish Fins   Tetrapod feet

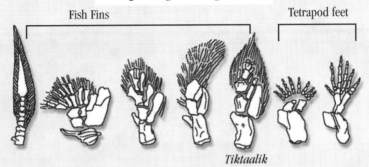

Tiktaalik

The fin diagram above shows a supposed morphological sequence of a fin becoming a foot from left to right. These are fins from actual fish that have been lined up into an evolutionary sequence. Look at it with critical eyes. Is the transition a smooth change from no finger like bones at the left to fingers at the right?

Find these items on the chart:
> The second fin from the left appears to show fingers
> Then the fourth fin shows no fingers at all
> Then Tiktaalik shows a few fingers
> Then there are suddenly a entire set of fingers

This does not appear to show a morphological sequence of fin to toes but goes back and forth between a toe, no toes, a few toes, then all toes.

The point of the diagram is to show a progression from a fin, to a fin with fingers, to finally a foot with toes. According to the diagram does this happen?   No!

To the creationist this diagram just shows the variation of types of fins in fish and then distinctly tetrapod hands as the last two fossils are arranged into an order to try and fit an evolutionary progression. However, there is no obvious progression from fin to toes or fingers.

Geologic sequence:

How are the fossils found in the rock layers? Are they found in the predicted order? The 'oldest' fossil should be found in the 'oldest' layer of rock (lower in the fossil record). The younger fossil should be found in a higher layer of rock.

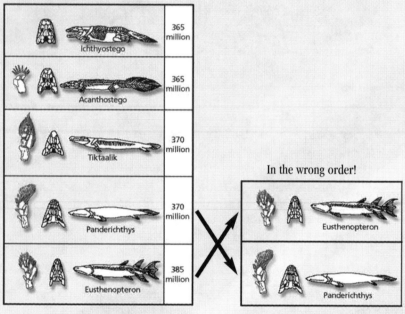

In the wrong order!

The left side of the diagram shows the table as the evolutionists have it arranged.

The right side of the diagram shows how the order of the arrangement is actually incorrect according to the evolutionary dates of the fossils

You can see that Panderichthys and Euthenopteron have traded positions. Panderichthys is supposedly 385 million years old while Eusthenopteron is 370 million years old. This is out of order on the chart!

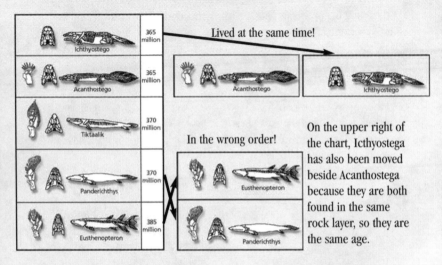

Lived at the same time!

In the wrong order!

On the upper right of the chart, Icthyostega has also been moved beside Acanthostega because they are both found in the same rock layer, so they are the same age.

We have shown that the evolutionist's geological sequence is not correct. When it is corrected, they are no longer in the right order for the evolutionary progression.

Acanthostega can not have evolved into Icthyostega because they lived at the same time.

Euthenopteron could not have evolved into Panderichthys because Panderichthys is supposedly older than Euthenopteron.

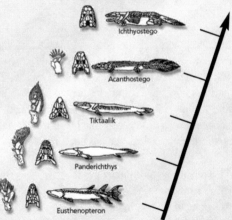

We discussed the problems with the order that the creatures are found in this evolutionary order. Draw arrows to rearrange the chart into the proper order. Explain the changes in your own words. Why is the order important?

A Summary

The evolutionary sequence of fish to tetrapods is not a very strong argument for the evolution of fish crawling onto land. The geological and morphological sequences are out of order. This suggests that this missing link is not a missing link at all but just another variety of fish!!

The special tetrapod attributes of Tiktaalik may actually help it for its special environment. It may have helped this fish to survive better in the shallow bottom of a river. The flat head enabled it to be covered in shallow water, and the fins with extra bones and strong ribs may have given it strength to prop itself when in those shallows. The lack of a bony gill cover might have given it more mobility. Although we can only make assumptions from its fossils about this fish, we do know that its special adaptations had a purpose given to it by the Creator.

But from the evolutionary perspective, when you look at the supposed evolutionary progression of the fin, there is no purpose. Why have bones evolved just to take them away in the next fish, and then to bring them back again? It just doesn't make sense.

Evolution of a Car

In this lesson, we've learned that we can line fish up into an sequence to make it appear as if they have evolved. We could do the same thing with the evolution of the car . . .

First I come across a wheel, in a junkyard.

Next I find an old bicycle with two wheels, and then a tricycle with three.

Then there's a little red wagon with four wheels.

Then I find an old Volkswagen Bug. Its design is simple, and the engine is in the back.

I look further and find a family car - the engine has improved and moved to the front.

Now I unearth a fast red sports car. It's aerodynamic, fast.

Taking all of these pieces I found in the junk-yard, I can line them up and show how a wheel gradually evolved into a red sports car.

The problem, is that cars didn't evolve! Each model was specially designed by an engineer. Likewise, a creationist points out that each fish and tetrapod is also designed by the Creator. But if I lined them up in the right way, could I make it look like they evolved?

Conclusion

Tiktaalik is an extraordinary fossil. The creationist interprets this fossil to be a fish that is highly specialized to its unique environment. Its tetrapod-like traits cause it to appear as a mosaic type of creature.

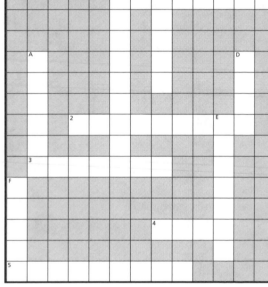

Cross word puzzle

DOWN

A) A type of art and a type of animal.
B) What is the name of the fossil fish?
C) There are _____ requirements for a evolutionary sequence
D) Tiktaalik is a type of _____-finned fish.
E) Just because two things have the same trait does not mean that they are

_____.

F) God created the original _____.

ACROSS

1) A _____ is an animal with four legs and a backbone.
2) What island did they find the fossil fish?
3) Which came first the chicken or the egg?
4) Evolutionists try to solve problems with more _____
5) Morphological change is a change in _____

Jonathan Park

Have you ever been scuba diving?

If you have, you have had the amazing privilege of looking into a whole other world that many people never get to see. You will have also felt the pressure of atmospheres being added to your surroundings. The deeper you go the more pressure, and the colder and darker the ocean world becomes.

Black smokers or hydrothermal vents are found much deeper than a human can dive. They are found at deep dark levels on the ocean floor. These vents were discovered in 1977. Some of the most famous hydrothermal vents are found at the Juan de Fuca ridge off of the Pacific Coast about 200 miles East of Seattle.

These Black smokers are found at a depth of about a mile beneath the ocean surface. Down there it truly is out of this world! Our Episode today takes us into this world through the cameras of a Remotely Operated Vehicle. How do life forms at these depths survive and where did they come from in the first place?

The very origin of life has, sadly, been a topic of vigorous speculation for hundreds of years, by those who have rejected the God of the Bible. The following drawings show some of those beliefs from the past about the beginning of life.

The Law of Biogenesis

Life can only come from life.

A long time ago people used to believe that non-living things could come alive. For example the ancient Egyptians used to believe that mice would form from the mud of the Nile River.

In 1600, Jan Baptist van Helmont created a "recipe" that he believed would produce mice. The formula? Dirty rags, cheese, and wheat in a jar for 21 days.

• Lid open

• Maggets on meat

• Gauze

• Maggets on gauze

• Sealed

• No Maggets

In 1668, another man named Fransisco Redi performed an experiment to prove that, contrary to the popular belief of his day, maggots were coming not from raw meat alone, but from flies laying eggs in the meat. He put meat in three jars. The first he left open. The second he covered with gauze, and the third he sealed tightly. Flies landed in the open jar and maggots appeared. On the second jar, flies landed on the gauze - and maggots appeared there, but not in the jar itself. In the sealed jar, there were no maggots whatsoever. This experiment proved that the maggots were coming from the flies, not the meat.

Another well known experiment was performed by Louis Pasteur in the 1800s. After boiling a broth, he placed it in flasks that would allow air to pass into the liquid but not any outside contaminants such as dust, bugs, etc. Nothing grew in the broth. Through this experiment, Mr. Pasteur proved that the living organisms were coming from outside contaminants, rather than from spontaneous generation within the liquid. This settled the issue. Life can only come from living things.

A law was then written to explain this concept. It is called the Law of Biogenesis. It says that life only comes from life.

Life has never been seen or shown to spontaneously generate or come out of dead things.

Traffic Laws & The Laws of Science

The laws of science are sort of like traffic laws, though you are not given a ticket if you break one!

What is a law?
A law is a rule that is not meant to be broken. Traffic laws help keep us safe. What are some traffic laws?

 STOP when the light is red.

 Obey the speed limit.

 Put on your blinker when turning

How does something in science become a law?
A scientific law starts as a theory and then becomes a law. They are, simply put, theories that have never been broken. For example, the Law of Biogenesis had many years of testing and experiments before it became a law. It has been found to be true without exception.

There are laws in each area of science.
- Laws of Chemistry
- Laws of Physics
- Laws of Biology

What is the law called that describes why everything that goes up must come down?

Yes! The Law of Gravity

This next section explains how evolutionary scientists try to break the Law of Biogenesis. They are doing experiments to try to create life from dead chemicals.

Evolutionary Origin of Life Theories

Because evolutionists say that chance has made life, the first life HAD to come about simply from chemicals. In this case, they go against the Law of Biogenesis and say that chemicals (something dead) came together to make the building blocks of life. They say that life came from non-life. Below are a few of their theories about how life was first created.

I'm ALIVE!!!

Here are some of the theories that have been proposed:

1. The first thing that scientists have to think about when it comes to the first life is the environment. What kind of environment would enable life to begin? They theorize that:
- The earth was very hot
- There was no oxygen in the atmosphere
- The liquid on the earth was not water but mostly chemicals and salts.

So ... the first life that randomly evolved had to be able to live in that environment. It had to be:
- **Anaerobic** - able to live without Oxygen.
- **Hyperthermophylic** - able to live in very high temperatures.
- **Halophylic** - salt and chemical loving.

Salt

Chemicals

High Temperatures

No Oxygen

2. The first environment created clay "bodies" where the first complex molecules formed. The clay bodies provided a place and materials for life to come together.

3. RNA was the first molecule that evolved because it can replicate itself.
   • RNA is made and used inside your cells to make copies of genetic material.

4. Another idea says that molecules began to interact in a cycle which produced more and more molecules, eventually becoming surrounded by a membrane, making the first cell.

5. Finally, Panspermia is the idea that life was created or evolved somewhere else in outerspace and then transported to earth.

The first theory seems to be the most popular, with maybe a combination of one or two of the other ideas added to it. There is a general consensus that high heat was part of the environment along with high chemical concentration and no light. Although all of these theories are interesting evolutionary speculation, there is no concrete evidence for any of them. As a matter of fact, these theories violate the scientific law that life can only come from life!

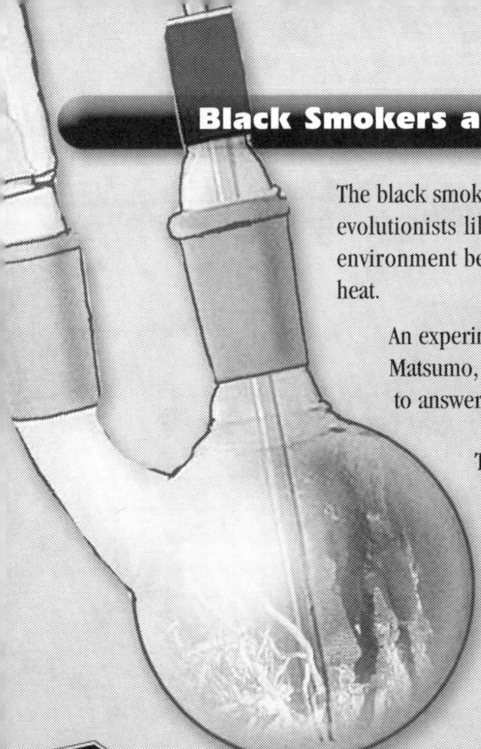

The black smokers are present day environments that evolutionists like as examples of the early earth environment because there are lots of chemicals and heat.

An experiment was designed by scientist named Matsumo, and others from Japan. They set out to answer a very interesting question:

The question: "Can amino acids be made to link together in a laboratory that mimics the black smoker environment?"

The experiment attempted to find a way to link amino acids into longer chains.

STOP

Wait a minute!!

What are amino acids?
They are the chemical parts that make up a cell.
    -They are a chemical molecule.
    -They are made of mostly hydrogen, oxygen, carbon, nitrogen, and sulfur.
    -There are 20 kinds.
    -They can link together to make a long chain.

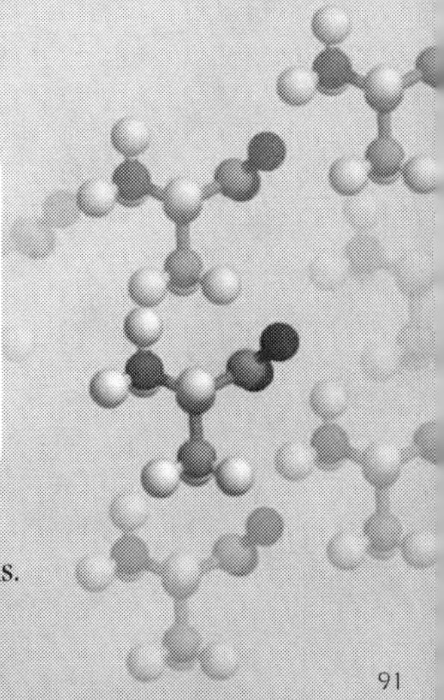

Forming chains of amino acids happens naturally in cells.

Important materials: The experiment used heat and amino acid solution.

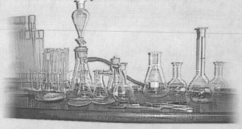

Results: They were able to simulate the coming together of amino acids to make more complex molecules like those needed to make life.

AHHHH Success!
Evolution is True!!!

But wait just a minute...

Problem: The experiment actually failed, because the heat would destroy the amino acids if they hadn't protected them right away! If their experiment hadn't been designed to protect the amino acids, they would have been gone before they could have ever become anything. The Law of Biogenesis remains unbroken!

The Black Smokers and The Life Found There

While evolutionists are trying to figure out if life could have evolved at the smokers, the fact is, there are some incredible creatures living there! The design of these wonderful animals tells us about the amazing design of the Creator.

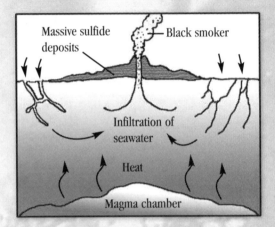

Black smokers are also called hydrothermal vents. They are cracks in the earth's crust on the bottom of the ocean that spew out very hot water and chemicals. When the hot water and chemicals meets the surrounding very cold water, it looks like hot, cloudy black smoke.

Interesting Facts:
- Temperature of surrounding sea water: near freezing 32 degrees F
- Temperature of vent water: 650-716 degrees F
- Chemical make-up: Iron, Zinc, Copper sulfides, Sulfates of Magnesium and Calcium.
- Depth of vent: around 1 mile deep

Creationists believe that black smokers are evidence of the worldwide flood. They show us the remnants of the fountains of the great deep that burst open to flood the earth, and the cooling off from the volcanic activity that would have caused the great fountains to open up.

Animals adapted to the life in the deep hotness!!

Animal highlights:

Tube worms

- These type of tube worms can grow up to 8 feet in length and 10 centimeters in diameter. They have a bright Red feathery plume.
- They are filter feeders and have special bacteria that live in their tissues to help them get food.

Mussels

- These type of mussels often grow larger than their relatives that live at the ocean surface. They also have special bacteria that live inside their gill tissues to help them get food.

Crabs

Brachyuran crabs live around vent sites in the Pacific Ocean. These round white crabs are predators. They eat bacteria, shrimp, mussels, clams, tubeworms, and each other.

Chemosynthesis

The black Smoker environment as stated earlier, is completely dark and filled with many chemicals.

How do animals live in that?

It has been discovered that a certain microbe called archaea can make energy or food by using the chemicals in the water.

These microbes are called chemoautotroughs because they can make their own food out of chemicals. They do this by a process called chemosynthesis.

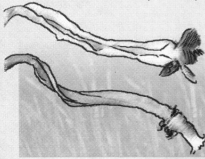

Inside the tubeworms, for example, live tons of the archaea.

The red plume of the tubeworm gathers oxygen and sulfide from the water. The chemicals then are gathered by the archaea which make food for the tubeworm. The tubeworm does NOT eat the archae but uses the energy it makes as its own.

How do land and other ocean animals get food?

I am sure that you have heard of the 'food chain'! Plants are called the primary producers of land and most ocean food chains. Through a process called photosynthesis, plants make their own food using the sun and then become food for others.

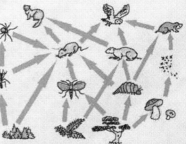

Write in your own words what the difference is between photosynthesis and chemosynthesis?

Designed adaptation

The animals that live around the black smoker environment are adapted uniquely to live in that environment. They live in:

High heat

Lots of chemical

No sunlight

Can you think of how these animals became adapted to live in this special place?

One reason is the design that God placed within the DNA of the animals that allowed them to change in order to live in this harsh place.

Activity

Compare a photosynthetic ocean food chain with a chemosynthetic food chain.

Copy and cut out the different figures on the page.

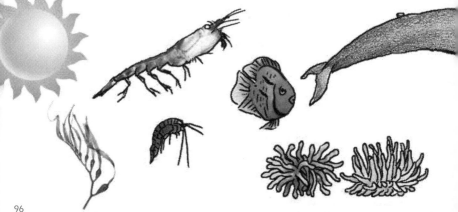

Recipe for GOOO!

Do an "Origin of Life" experiment in your own kitchen!

1. Mix together 2 tablespoons of white glue and 2 tablespoons of water.

2. In another container, mix together ten drops of your choice of food coloring, 1/4 cup of water, and 3/4 teaspoon of borax laundry detergent.

3. Add 2 tablespoons of the borax mixture to the glue mixture and stir well.

4. Play with your Goo. Store it in an airtight container. Do not eat it! And if you notice any lifeforms beginning to grow in it, throw it away!

Make two food chains, one photosynthetic and one chemosynthetic.
Glue the figures in the correct order of each chain as if one organism would be eating the next. Place the primary producers on the bottom and go up from there.

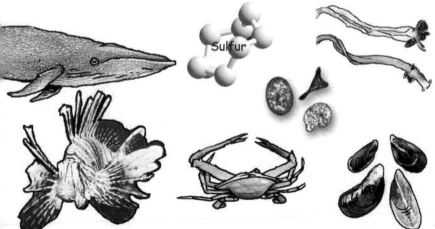

Origin of Life Dilemmas

Do you know what a dilemma is? It is when you are simultaneously presented with two solutions, both which don't seem to be very good options. When it comes to many of the "origin of life" theories, they seem to require opposite conditions at the same time:

Dilemma 1

First, Evolutionists have a dilemma with the issue of heat. In their "origin of life" experiments, it seems to be required to make and join amino acids, but this same heat also destroys them.

In the lab, scientists draw the amino acids out of the heated solution to preserve them before the heat that made them also destroys them. However, would this happen in a natural environment? No. The amino acids would be destroyed before they could arrange themselves into the building blocks needed for life.

Oh no! My amino acid is burned again.

Dilemma 2

Evolutionists then have another dilemma with the amino acids they can make in their experiments.

In the lab, two types of amino acids are always created by their experiments. They are said to be right and left handed amino acids.

However, ONLY left handed amino acids are found in living things. Right-handed amino acids wreck the amino chains! Since they are unable to create results from their experiments that only produce left handed amino acids their experiments fail.

Amino acids do not really have left and right hands! This just refers to their special shape.

You're right-handed, but you don't know anything about life.

Dilemma 3

Evolutionists also have a dilemma with oxygen. In the lab, oxygen is NOT included in the experiments because it would destroy the molecules they are trying to make! Why? Because the chemical oxygen reacts negativelywith many of the other chemicals, so evolutionists leave oxygen out of their experiments.

The only problem is that, as soon as a cell is created, it requires oxygen to live. So if life really could be created in conditions like in their experiments, there would both need to be oxygen - and can't be oxygen at the same time! It is impossible!

Oxygen? No!
Oxygen? Yes!
Oxygen? No!
Oxygen? Yes!

Dilemma 4

Finally, evolutionists have a dilemma with the ingredients needed to make amino acids.

They need formaldehyde, hydrogen cyanide, and sugars to artificially create the amino acids. The problem? These things are destructive and poisonous to the life forms they're trying to make - and would kill them right away, assuming that they could even be made in the first place!

Origin of Life Experiments

In the last section, we mentioned a Japanese "origin of life" experiment that tried to show how life might have formed at an environment similar to a black smoker.

Following are descriptions of a few other experiments:

Miller-Urey Experiment

Question: Could an evolutionary atmosphere provide the conditions needed for making life?

Materials Used: methane, ammonia, hydrogen

Procedure: An electric spark was used as energy for the reactions. They set-up a trap to collect the products made in the experiment so that the next spark would not destroy them.

Results: 85% Tar, 15% Carbonic acid and only 2% amino acids -- both left and right handed amino acids (remember it must be only left handed for life).

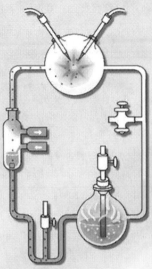

Creation Analysis

The Miller experiment used gasses that were thought to be the same as those in the earth's early atmosphere, but of course Miller did not include oxygen.

The electric spark was meant to simulate something like lightning flashing into the early earth's atmosphere to give the energy needed to make chemicals combine. Miller made a special 'trap' to collect and save the new chemicals so that the next spark would not also destroy the new products of the reaction.

The scientists had made amino acids, and for some people this fact is enough. However, the problem is that not only were these amino acids artificially saved in the trap, but biological molecules are ONLY made of left handed amino acids. The experiment failed to show how life could be made from non-living chemicals!

Sidney Fox Experiment

Question: Can life come from non-life?

Materials Used: amino acids

Procedure: Amino acids were heated to 347 degrees F, and then mixed with water. Finally, the product was filtered to gain the desired results.

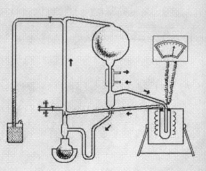

Results: The experiment produced linked chains of left and right handed amino acids.

Creation Analysis

From the analysis of the Miller experiment that we just talked about, can you figure out the dilemmas for this experiment?

Just making amino acids or joining a couple together is not making life. There is a huge difference between forming amino acids and the actual genetic material of DNA. DNA is an incredible molecule.

> Abilities of DNA:
> Read
> Proofread
> Repairs itself
> Duplicates
> Transcribes
> Translates a chemical code into our physical body.

Experiments that try to make life in a test tube have many problems. Amino acids and DNA are just too complicated and incredibly detailed. It does not seem logical to say that random chance accidents could bring about the right chemicals to create life! Even more, it violates the Law of Biogenesis. A better explanation is to say that it was designed by the Creator.

Many origin of life experiments assume that the early earth did not have any oxygen in it. If this assumption is true, we should see no evidence of it in the geologic rocks.

Scientists look for two types of rock. One is called hematite and the other is called pyrite. Both of these rocks contain iron. Hematite is made when oxygen is present. Pyrite is made when oxygen is NOT present.

Have you ever seen a rusty nail? Some nails are made of a metal called iron.

The rust on a nail is caused when oxygen is added to the iron. A rusty nail is going through a slow process called oxidation.

Hematite rock goes through a similar process when oxygen is added to it. The process makes the rock red like the rust on a nail.

So when you find a red hematite rock-you can assume oxygen was in the air when it was formed.

What is the point?

Scientists use this information to see if there was evidence for oxygen in the earth's atmosphere when life was first forming. Scientists DO find hematite in the oldest known rocks, Precambrian. What does this mean? Oxygen was present in the earth's atmosphere. So the idea that there was once an atmosphere without oxygen doesn't fit the evidence from geology.

Difference between creation and evolution perspectives

It all comes down to this:

Evolution and creation theories relate to how we live our lives. They have opposite implications.

Evolution	Creation
If we live out the evolutionary philosophy, we believe that all things are made by accident. **Implication:** No reason or purpose for life.	If we live out a creation worldview, we come to understand that all things are designed with a reason. **Implication:** My life has ultimate purpose.

One of the points of being a follower of Christ is to discover your specific purpose that God designed for you.

One way you find your purpose is through putting on the things of Christ -- the armor of God.

"¹⁰Finally, my brethren, be strong in the Lord, and in the power of his might. ¹¹Put on the whole armour of God, that ye may be able to stand against the wiles of the devil. ¹²For we wrestle not against flesh and blood, but against principalities, against powers, against the rulers of the darkness of this world, against spiritual wickedness in high places. ¹³Wherefore take unto you the whole armour of God, that ye may be able to withstand in the evil day, and having done all, to stand. ¹⁴Stand therefore, having your loins girt about with truth, and having on the breastplate of righteousness; ¹⁵And your feet shod with the preparation of the gospel of peace." - Ephesians 6:10-15

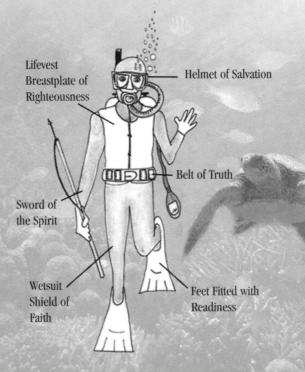

Lifevest
Breastplate of
Righteousness

Helmet of Salvation

Belt of Truth

Sword of
the Spirit

Wetsuit
Shield of
Faith

Feet Fitted with
Readiness

Jonathan Park

In these episodes, the JP team travels to Germany to a place called Langenberg Quarry, near the town of Goslar. The mountain range pictured below, called the Harz mountains, is where many of the fossils discussed in these two adventures are found.

In the northern part of the Harz mountains of Germany, a discovery was made in 1998 of a miniature dinosaur called Europasaurus holgeri (we'll refer to it as "Hanna," its original nickname, from now on). They were a type of sauropod that is only one fifth of the size of their full-grown counterparts-such as Brachiosaurus which was around 82 feet long and 42 feet high. The size of a Hanna ranges from 5 to 20 feet in total body length.

Brachiosaurus

Europasarus holgeri

Artist's rendition of Europasaurus holgeri

Dinosaur Extinction

What happened to the dinosaurs?
There are many different theories of extinction that evolutionists propose:

Was it a giant meteor impact that killed them?

Was it a radical climate change?

Did disease wipe them out?

Evolutionists have over a hundred dinosaur extinction theories.

Can you come up with a good theory?

Creationists would propose that Noah's Flood killed most of the dinosaurs, but Noah would have brought some on the ark along with the other animals.

So the flood would not have been the cause of their extinction. But after the flood, the climate would have changed so dramatically that they many not have been able to adapt and so became extinct.

There is evidence that the earth was inundated with water. One of the evidences having to do with dinosaurs and water are called fossil graveyards.

What are fossil graveyards?

Fossil graveyards are not organized places having tombstones labeling each thing buried.

Fossil graveyards are a jumbled mess of bones ripped apart by the water's power and swept together and buried together.

There are many fossil graveyards around the world, such as in the Tenere desert of Niger known for its extensive fossil graveyard, and Ghost ranch, discussed in previous episodes.

Dinosaur graveyards around the world show evidence that the dinosaurs were buried in watery conditions.

Evolutionists would say that each different site was a local flood - or ancient river - or sea. But if there's evidence of a flood at dinosaur sites all around the world, then it may be excellent proof for a worldwide flood!

Water Has Power!

How is water able to do so much damage as rip bones apart and make graveyards? Have you experienced a flood from a river, rain, or even a tidal wave?

One reason that water has so much power is the turbulent currents produced as it flows.

Another reason is it sticks together.

The 'stickyness' gives it a particular amount of viscosity.

A solution that is really viscous is honey. It is thick and takes a long time to pour onto your pancakes.

Although water is less viscous than honey, its viscosity is perfect for its purposes and also contributes to its destructive power.

Rivers have many different currents and turbulence. The surface of a flowing river may look calm but underneath there are rocks, logs, and other obstacles that contribute to a chaotic current.

Turbulence is a chaotic, changing current flow, moving really fast.

This is turbulence from a tip of an airplane wing. This type of turbulence can also happen underwater.

The turbulent force of water can easily rip things apart.

Activity: Testing Turbulence

The best way to test turbulence is to find a small local stream and do some wading.

Look for areas where logs or rocks stick into the stream and observe the current created by the objects.

Notice the smooth parts, the bubbly parts, and the jumbled parts.

A new current is made when you put your feet in the water. Your legs force the water to go around your legs causing a new swirling current.

Use your observation skill to observe the water currents.

What's the point?

Creationists and evolutionists both agree that water is an important ingredient in making fossils and in forming the earth's crust. But they both interpret its meaning in different ways.

Difference between evolution model and creation

Evolutionists look at the area of Germany and interpret in this way:

150 million years ago many parts of Germany were underwater. We find large deposits of marine fossils and water deposited sediments.

During this period, there were several small islands poking out from the sea. This particular spot is thought to be close to one of those islands.

Evolutionists believe that these miniature dinosaurs were living on the island, died, and were transported off the island by a river, and buried in shallow water and then fossilized.

Creationists would look at this same area and interpret it this way:

Germany was under water at some time possibly because of the worldwide flood. The marine fossils and water deposited sediments are also evidence for this.

The Dwarf Dinosaurs

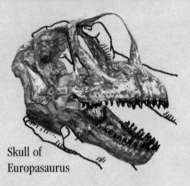

Skull of
Europasaurus

What do we mean by dwarf dinosaurs?

Do you think that you would like to have one for a pet? Even though they are called dwarf doesn't mean that they are very small. Notice the picture below that shows you how big a full grow Europasaurus holgeri is. That is pretty big!

Why is it such a big deal that these dinosaurs are dwarfs? Let's find out!

Scientists first thought that they were young dinosaurs because of their size.

But after looking at 11 different specimens more closely, they found growth indicators that showed that they were actually full grown.

Scientists compared the leg bone tissues of a typical large-bodied sauropod, Camarasaurus, and concluded that the smaller size of Europasaurus resulted from a decreased growth rate.

How could there be such a huge variation in size from 3 tons to 15 tons?

First let's look at horses.

The Falabella horse is the smallest breed of horse in the world, reaching around 30 inches in size.

These horses illustrate that a size variety range can be seen today. These horse breeds were made by selecting small size horses and breeding them together through a series of generations.

In the natural world this variation can also be seen, but it happens in a different way:

A group of animals usually live together in a particular habitat.

Then, a few smaller animals may move away together looking for food because they can't compete with the bigger animals for food.

Then, something happens that keeps them from returning to their original habitat.

NOW the animals are isolated from the original group.

Because of the isolation they can only breed between themselves. This can cause hidden genes to come out.

So when the small animals breed together they make more small animals so the whole population will be small as long as they remain isolated from the original group.

The Bare Bones: Catastrophic Deposition of the Dinosaurs

When we look at dinosaur graveyards like the Langenberg Quarry in Germany, we can observe that the bones are not nicely laid in a grave as we talked about earlier. And this supports a worldwide flood.

The evidence: The bones are disarticulated.

Disarticulation means that the bones are all separated from each other and from any tissues that would hold them together.

Only force would cause disarticulation. Forces tore the creatures apart before they were buried.

The evidence: The bones are well preserved.

There are no signs of decay or predators eating the bones so they were quickly deposited and buried.

The conclusion: the force and the preservation indicate that a catastrophic type of water and sediment force was at work to make these fossils and possibly kill the animals in the first place.

Where do Creation and Evolution Differ?

Evolutionists say that there was a local flood of a river that carried animal bones, buried them by sediments and fossilized.

Creationists would say that the catastrophe is the worldwide flood.

Proof for Violent Deposition

There are three evidences that support the creation concepts for a violent flood:

- **Interclasts**
- **Carbonate Mudstone**
- **Variety of animals**

Interclasts

Interclasts are a specific type rock that belongs to rocks that are called clastic sedimentary rocks.

Clastic are a type of rock that are made up from broken pieces of other rocks called clasts that have all been reformed back together.

Chocolate-chip nut cookies resemble a clastic rock. They have chunks and pieces (clasts) mixed in with the cookie dough.

The fact that clastic rocks are present around the fossils is evidence for turbulence, which means that they were made with strong forces of water.

Interpretation:

Evolution says that the fossils were deposited in a calm, shallow sea, but the presence of clasts contradicts this idea because to make clastic rock, violent water turbulence is needed.

Creation interprets this to indicate that there was a strong flood.

Carbonate mudstone

This area is also covered in carbonate mudstone deposited in water. Along with this there are many marine fossils. Carbonate rocks are a type of sedimentary rock made of carbonate minerals.

Mudstone is a fine-grained sedimentary rock who came from clays or muds. It is a mix of silt and clay sized particles.

The point of carbonate mud-stone is that it is only deposited in the presence of water.

Interpretation:

Evolution states that the area was covered by a sea.

Creation states that the area was covered by the waters of the flood.

Variety of Animals

There is an incredible variety of fossil animals found at this site.

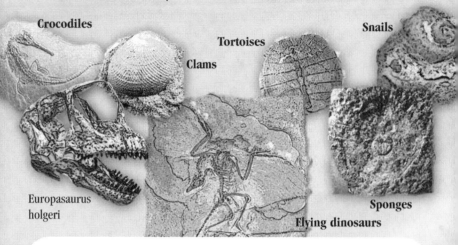

Crocodiles

Tortoises

Clams

Snails

Europasaurus holgeri

Sponges

Flying dinosaurs

Could all of these animals live in the same ecosystem? Why or why not?

_____

What type of habitat does a sponge live in?

_____

What type of habitat does a crocodile live in?

_____

Why is it so amazing that the fossils of a sponge and a crocodile are found in the same area?

_____

Why is it even more amazing that all those animals are found in the same area?

_____

Fossil graveyards arise because of many factors: presence of water, power and force of water, chemical make-up of the sediments, and other factors. The graveyards are one part of the evidence that supports the creation model. The other pieces of evidence discussed were: Well preserved disarticulated fossils, clastic rock, carbonate mudstone, and the variety of fossils animals in the graveyards.

Use your understanding of all the things you learned in these two episodes to do the next exercise. By looking at the drawings, use the list of evidence to figure out what scenario best fits the evidence by looking for it in the drawing.

List of evidence:

Well preserved disarticulated fossils   Carbonate mudstone
Clastic rock   Variety of fossil animals

Matching Game

Match the animal with its ecosystem by drawing a line.

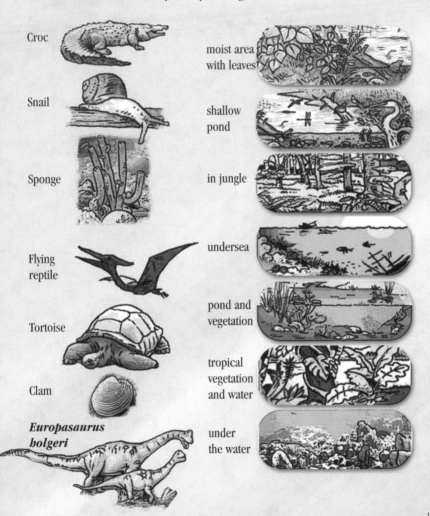

Croc	moist area with leaves
Snail	shallow pond
Sponge	in jungle
Flying reptile	undersea
Tortoise	pond and vegetation
Clam	tropical vegetation and water
Europasaurus holgeri	under the water

Fill in the blank

Write the letter E (meaning evolution) or C (meaning creation) in the space provided to show if the evidence is part of the creation or evolution theory.

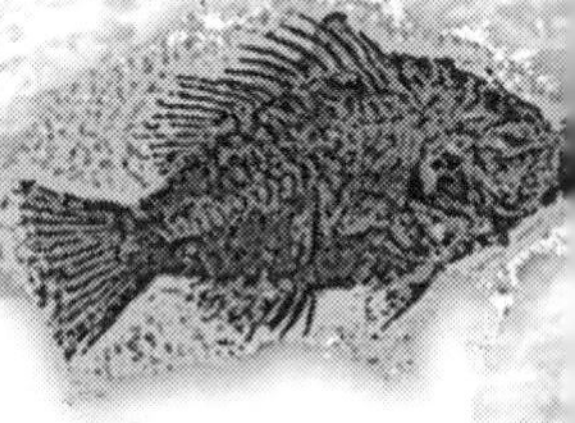

_____ Well preserved fossils

_____ Carbonate mudstone

_____ Disarticulated fossils

_____ Variety of fossil animals

_____ Clastic rock

_____ River

_____ Clam sea